THE GOD
OF CHRISTIA

VOLL £3.50

Liberation and Theology Series

Editorial Committee
Leonardo Boff, Sergio Torres, Gustavo Gutiérrez,
José Comblin, Ronaldo Muñoz, Enrique Dussel,
José Oscar Beozzo, Pedro Trigo, Ivone Gebara,
Jon Sobrino, Virgil Elizondo, Juan Luis Segundo

Ecumenical Consultant
Julio de Santa Ana

. . . "this is going to be a series which both illuminates Latin American realities and provokes thought about the relevance to the rest of the world of a theology which springs very powerfully out of these realities – out of the people's suffering and out of a still vibrant faith." — David L. Edwards, *The Church Times*

Ronaldo Muñoz

THE GOD
OF CHRISTIANS

*Translated from the Spanish by
Paul Burns*

BURNS & OATES

First published in this translation in Great Britain in 1991
by Burns & Oates Ltd, Wellwood, North Farm Road,
Tunbridge Wells, Kent TN2 3DR
and in the United States of America
by Orbis Books, Maryknoll, New York 10545

Published originally in Spain by Ediciones Paulinas, Madrid,
under the title *Dios de los Cristianos*.
Revised edition published in Chile
by Ediciones Paulinas – Chile in 1988.

Original edition © CESEP – São Paulo and Ediciones Paulinas, 1987

English Translation © Burns & Oates/Search Press 1991

ISBN 0 86012 173 9

Typeset in the U.S.A. from translator's computer disk
Printed and bound in Great Britain by
Biddles Ltd, Guildford and King's Lynn

Liberation and Theology Series

In the years since its emergence in Latin America, liberation theology has challenged the church to a renewal of faith lived in solidarity with the poor and oppressed. The effects of this theology have spread throughout the world, inspiring in many Christians a deeper life or faith and commitment, but for others arousing fears and concerns.

Its proponents have insisted that liberation theology is not a sub-topic of theology but really a new way of doing theology. The Liberation and Theology Series is an effort to test that claim by addressing the full spectrum of Christian faith from the perspective of the poor.

Thus, volumes in the Series are devoted to such topics as God, Christ, the Church, Revelation, Mary, the Sacraments, and so forth. But the Series will also explore topics seldom adressed by traditional theology, though vital to Christian life – aspects of politics, culture, the role of women, the status of ethnic minorities. All these are examined in the light of faith lived in a context of oppression and liberation.

The work of over a hundred theologians, pastoral agents, and social scientists from Latin America, and supported by some one hundred and forty bishops, the Liberation and Theology Series is the most ambitious and creative theological project in the history of the Americas.

Addressed to the universal church, these volumes will be essential reading for all those interested in the challenge of faith in the modern world. They will be especially welcomed by all who are committed to the cause of the poor, by those engaged in the struggle for a new society, by all those seeking to establish a more solid link between faith and politics, prayer and action.

"This is a most enterprising series which should enable those of us who live in the West to listen to what the liberation theologians themselves have to say. It may well open the eyes of Western Christians to the need for liberation in the First World as well." – *The Expository Times*

To the memory of my grandmother
Fidelicia Salinas
who taught me to know
the God of the poor

Contents

vii

PART THREE
BIBLICAL REFLECTION

I am the God of your fathers, the God of Abraham, the God of Isaac, and the God of Jacob. . . . I have seen the humiliation of my people in Egypt and I hear their cry. . .

Exodus 3:6–7

Woman . . . go to my brothers and say to them: I am ascending to my Father, who is your Father, to my God, who is your God.

John 20:17

The church seeks to ask young people a key question: "Who is your God?" It knows that the answer to this question involves the meaning of life, of the world, of history. It is therefore impossible to relegate this question to the private sphere of people's lives.

The Bishops of Chile
Pastoral Orientations 1986–9, no. 39

Preface

This is a book written with sweat, tears and joy.

It has three parts, which I hope complement each other and follow one from another: The first — narrative — introduces the subject as it affects us (mainly the poor of the Third World) today, and gives a reasoned account of our recent journey with God.

The second — systematic — deals with some of the main questions we ask of God, those that have always been asked, but in the way they are being asked by the poor, and especially the young, today.

The third — biblical — tries to close the circle with a faithful and "feet-on-the-ground" reading of the word of this same God, as given to us in the biblical story culminating in Jesus Christ.

I owe a greater debt than they can realize to my neighbours and the Christian community of the township of Malaquias Concha for their help and inspiration; to the lay theologian Raul Rosales for his constant companionship and valued suggestions; to Victor Soto and Carlos Lange for their preparation of the typescript.

Abbreviations and Short Forms

AG   *Ad Gentes.* Vatican II, Decree on the Church's Missionary Activity

CELAM   Conference of Bishops of Latin America

CLAR   Confederation of Latin American Religious

DS   Denzinger-Schönmetzer. *Enchiridion Symbolorum, definitionum et declarationum de rebus fidei et morum.* First published 1854, latest edition 1976

DV   *Dei Verbum.* Vatican II, Dogmatic Constitution on Divine Revelation

GS   *Gaudium et Spes.* Vatican II, Pastoral Constitution on the Church in the Modern World

JB   *The Jerusalem Bible*

Medellín   Second General Conference of Latin American Bishops, held in Medellín, Colombia, in 1968. Translations of the final documents are in vol. 2 of *The Church in the Present-day Transformation of Latin America.* Washington, D.C.: USCC, 1970

PL   *Patrologiae Cursus Completus, Series Latina.* Ed. J. P. Migne. Paris, 1844–1855

Puebla   Third General Conference of Latin American Bishops, held in Puebla, Mexico, in 1979. A translation of the "Final Document" can be found in J. Eagleson and P. Scharper, eds., *Puebla and Beyond.* Maryknoll, N.Y.: Orbis, 1980; also in *Puebla.* Slough: St Paul; London: CIIR, 1980

REB   *Revista Eclesiástica Brasileira.* Petrópolis, Brazil

RH   *Redemptor Hominis.* Pope John Paul II, Encyclical Letter

RLT   *Revista Latinoamericana de Teología.* San Salvador

PART ONE

THE GOD OF THE POOR

CHAPTER I

The Subject of God

1. THE PARTICULAR SUBJECT OF THIS BOOK

All "theology," as the word itself implies, deals with God.[1] All "Christian" theology deals with God starting from the self-communication our faith tells us that God has made in Jesus, the "Christ." Jesus of Nazareth, who suffered under Pontius Pilate, forms part of our world and our history as human beings. We have to understand him in the context of his world and his age, and in the context of a history that preceded him and continues down to us.

Our faith in Jesus Christ and in the witness to God he left us gives the ultimate meaning and hope to us, to the world and to the collective history we live here and now. This means that everything that truly concerns our life and our history as human beings can be the subject of "theology."[2] It also means that our knowledge of the God of Jesus Christ—as the distinct and central "object" of the Christian faith and of any consistent, Christian theological undertaking—does not reach us separately from our own reality and human hopes, those we share in history here and now.

This means that, while we learn constantly from the theological tradition of the past, and from what people all over the world believe today, we also have to listen to "what the Spirit is saying to the churches" in the part of the world in which we live, which, writing from Latin America, is essentially a world in

which the majority of the people are both believing and poor.
So we have to look for a language about God that speaks to this
experience and the challenges it brings.[3] The three quotes, two
biblical and one contemporary, placed at the front of this book
indicate the approach to be taken here in speaking of that God
and Father of Jesus Christ, who speaks to us in our history and
gives us life through the Spirit.

2. THE PARADOX OF ALL THEO-LOGY

Theology, then, is reflection on, knowledge of and speaking
(*logia*) about God (*ho Theos*). But can we really make God an
object of our reflection, knowledge and speech?

Not, certainly, in the sense in which the "positive" natural
sciences understand the words—putting forward hypotheses,
devising experiments, measuring and calculating. This is not,
either, the way we understand human life in its basic humanness,
what we call the life of the spirit: understanding, love, freedom;
nor is it, to be more precise, how we understand material life,
working and living together, insofar as these are informed by
understanding, love and freedom. And God is, we say, life and
spirit par excellence. So if we know that human life, in its essential humanness, surpasses our precise categories and calculations, this has to be even more true of God.[4]

Why is this so?

In the first place, because God is total; because, if God is
God, we are from the outset "in" God: "In God we live, breathe,
and have our being." Everything in our lives and history speaks
to us of God, refers us back to God. God sustains all that is
innermost to us; we long for and seek God, consciously or not,
in all our anxieties and aspirations. This in itself makes it difficult to picture God: we cannot make God into an "object" in
the scientific sense of the word, something we can place in front
of ourselves, to examine its contours and understand it intellectually.

In the second place, because we experience our encounter
with God as a radical happening; because, if we have indeed
"encountered" God in any way, we are left with an intuition of
life and spirit more intense than anything we can conceive on

the basis of our meetings with other human beings. This intuition is of a sovereign "subject" of love and freedom, which rules out any idea of taking God "by surprise," of making God an object of our study and questioning. On the contrary, God can be known "personally" only insofar as God takes the initiative, comes to meet us and takes us by surprise, shows us what God is in the freedom of totally sovereign and gratuitous love. That is, God can be known personally only insofar as we allow ourselves to be surprised and radically questioned by God; as we respond to this intensely personal love, placing our lives entirely in God's hands and committing ourselves entirely to God's plans.

In the third place, because God is the transcendent one; because however much we are "in" God from the outset, however much God comes to meet us in our history, God is and always will be greater. God can impregnate and sustain everything, can decide to communicate personally with us, but is always "before" us and all our concerns, always "beyond" everything that is. We belong to God and can know the gift of God's personal love, but God does not belong to our world, like one more being in it, however much we try to place God as the basic and supreme being. We cannot understand God in our categories, cannot grasp God's thoughts, or involve God in our plans. If we are not to deceive ourselves and reduce God's image to an empty idol, we have to recognize in all honesty that, beyond everything that is human, God is and always will be God. We must do this in all honesty, and also in the deepest joy, since it is only on these conditions that we allow God to be our liberator, in the fullest and most surprising sense of the word.[5]

Hence the paradox for all authentic "theo-logy": that God (*ho Theos*) is the major "subject" of our lives and our witness as believers, while at the same time—through being essentially total, radical and transcendent—God is the least objectifiable, the least circumscribable subject in the framework or categories of our rational discourse (*logia*). We have to engage this subject with the best of our capacity for understanding and explaining, while knowing from the outset that all our discursive efforts will remain basically inadequate, will be meaningful only as a stage in or dimension of the humble and committed welcome of faith.

3. HISTORICAL THEO-LOGY, IN HOPE

The fact is that the experience of God as God—total, radical and transcendent—is being actualized and renewed for us in our collective history. This process starts from what we suffer, what we long for and what we are winning as a people. It begins when we are most conscious of journeying as an oppressed people, a journey in which there are also signs of life, struggle in solidarity and hope.

The history of the oppressed on their way to liberation is not the only focal point or dimension of our lives where we know the presence or suffer the absence of God. But it is true that it is in this history, as a collective journey, that God now seems to come to meet us in the most pressing manner; it is here that we today either experience the presence of God's life most intensely or feel the scandal of God's absence most acutely.[6]

The God we rediscover and go on seeking in this history is none other than the God of Jesus Christ, the same God whom Jesus of Nazareth knew better than anyone and to whom he bore witness with his oppressed people in the history of his time; the same God his people had experienced in their collective history since the days of the exodus from Egypt, and, farther back, since the patriarchs who wandered through the lands of the promise. This is the God to whom "our fathers cried," as the Psalms tell us, the God who heard Jesus' cry in his agony (Heb. 5:7), the God to whom all the oppressed peoples of Latin America are now crying.[7] The whole Bible is in effect the story of this God's self-revelation to a particular people in the course of their own history, that of an oppressed people on their way to liberation. And it is in the light of this biblical word that we can discover this same God in the collective history we are going through today.[8]

This God has been revealed to us "once and for all" in the actions, words and very person of Jesus Christ (see DV 4) "in the days of his mortal life" (Heb. 5:7), at the time when Pontius Pilate was governor in Judea. But the God whom Jesus Christ reveals to us is not one who can be contained in a system of law or dogma; rather this God is the creator who "goes on working"

(John 5:17) till now, the Lord who "from age to age . . . has acted with power [to] put down the mighty from their thrones and lift up those who are downtrodden" (Luke 1:49–52), the God of the Kingdom, which we pray will "come" to our society on earth, the God whose will—of bread and shared forgiveness—we pray may be done "this day."

This is the God who has been revealed to us in Jesus Christ and whom we come to know through experience in our history as oppressed and believing peoples. But this revelation and knowledge are given to us only in the shadow of faith. The very disciples who accompanied Jesus in the flesh, who "ate and drank with him after his resurrection from the dead" (Acts 10:41), were still left hungering to "see the Father" (see John 14:6–11), since "no one has ever seen God." Although we have been given the Spirit who assures us that we are children of God, although through our practice of shared love we can "know" that God is present, sharing the journey of the people of God, yet "at present, we see dimly, as in a faulty mirror" (1 Cor. 13:12).

All Christian knowledge of God is experience and meeting, but of and with a God who remains hidden, who is always beyond, waiting for us in the future. This experience and meeting are those of a pilgrim people, always on a quest for the promised fullness of freedom and life.

Our God is the God of human beings, who has come close to us in Jesus Christ; but this same God will finally become familiar to each and all of us when we as human beings reach the maturity of our head, the risen Christ (see Eph. 4:13–16). Our God takes the part of the downtrodden of the earth, is the God of the Kingdom promised to the poor, to those who hunger and thirst for justice, who work to build peace (see Matt. 5:1–12), but we shall know this God fully as "God in us" only once the downtrodden have been set free and the fullness of the Kingdom has come, once God has come to "wipe every tear from our eyes," so that "there shall be no more death or mourning, crying out or pain" (Rev. 21:3–4). Our God is at the same time the universal Father, who gives life to all and wills the salvation of just and sinners alike (see Matt. 5:43–8), but we shall see this God as "all in all" only at the end, when all injus-

tice and death itself have been destroyed, and humanity and the
world fully reconciled (see Isa. 11:1–9; 1 Cor. 14:24–8; Rom.
8:18–25).

So, God is still and will go on being for us the God of the
future, the God to come, whom we hope to meet and know
completely in the promised *pleroma*. Meanwhile, our experience
of faith and our theo-logy are no more than a fleeting sketch,
made in the hope of the meeting to come.

Both our theology and our faith need to keep their feet firmly
on the ground, consciously sharing in present history from "the
perspective of the poor."[9] They also need — as the Fathers said
of the church — "eyes to the front and the back," looking forward
to the God who is to come and fixed on the past of God in their
history, looking ahead toward seeing the Father "face to face"
while fixed also on the event accomplished in Jesus Christ. (Here
we need to beware of two reductionist interpretations, both
removed from the biblical tradition and from our experience as
believers. The first is the "mystic" interpretation of Platonic
stamp, which sees this future meeting as something concerning
the soul only after death, detached from the body, from the
human community and from history. The second is the "utopic"
Marxist interpretation, which sees the future fullness as a reign
of freedom and human solidarity that will occur in collective
history without any break from the present condition of humankind. In the first, bodily life and human community, the world
and history, are deprived of meaning; in the second, each human
being with his or her personal destiny is deprived of value. The
authentic Christian tradition, by contrast, makes no separation
between the personal and the communal, the spiritual and the
earthly. Our eschatological hope — based on the word and resurrection of Jesus Christ — is that we shall each find our "face
to face" and fullness of life with God in rising with Christ, going
beyond our personal death, and that this same resurrection of
ours will consist in sharing the fullness of the Kingdom, of the
"new creation," the place where justice will reign.)[10]

It is the Holy Spirit who enables us believers to keep our eyes
to the front and the back. The Spirit recalls, communicates and
interprets the story, word and life itself of Jesus Christ, which
are both witness to the Father and communication of the God

of life. The same Spirit also guides us toward the complete truth; it is given to us as the firstfruits of the full life we shall share with the risen Christ, an anticipation of the Father's inheritance already enjoyed by the firstborn of a host of brothers and sisters (see John 16:13; Rom. 8:9–30).[11]

4. THE RELEVANCE OF THE SUBJECT OF GOD

The God of Jesus Christ is the living centre and final goal of our faith, the central and ultimate "object" of all Christian theology. This has always been so and always must be. In the churches of Latin America, though, there is now a growing conviction that the subject of God, the specific and critical treatment of this subject, has acquired a sharp and pressing historical relevance.[12]

On this "Christian continent," the privileged minorities use the name of God as they fight with all the weapons of power and technology to defend their property and civilization; at the same time the majorities use the name of God as they try to live human lives in inhuman conditions and struggle just to survive the daily depredations of impoverishment. And within these same impoverished majorities, most resign themselves to their destitution and subjection in the name of God, though a growing number are awakening and organizing for a struggle for collective liberation, also in the name of God.

In the majority Catholic Church and other mainstream churches, some use the name of God and the mission received from Jesus Christ to urge solidarity with the impoverished masses, making taking their side in the struggle for a more just world the all-important task. Others, also in the name of God and their mission, stress the formulas of orthodoxy and worship, religious proselytism and internal church discipline as all-important. Finally, there is a "political centre" which uses the name of God to call for social reconciliation, not paying too much attention to the "devastating results of the Marxist cancer," but on the other hand not really seeming to give due weight to the age-old marginalization from which the oppressed people suffer.

Faced with such a discrepancy of approaches, one has to ask whether God — as God — really matters "above all things," or whether we are merely taking the name of God in vain, as a symbol to legitimize our personal or group interests, as one more—and very powerful—weapon in this real ideological war that rages amongst us. We urgently need to undertake a thorough critical review of our "good faith" as believers: as individuals, facing up to our pride and our fears; as a group or class, facing up to our collective reactions and interests, our more or less unconscious myths and ideologies.

But we need to go beyond this effort at self-examination, indispensable though it is, and ask ourselves in all seriousness how far the image of God we hold in "good faith" truly corresponds to the God of Jesus Christ. This is not only the prime theological question; it is also the basic determinant of the "Christianity" of our faith.

Clearly, if all these different groups can honestly uphold, in the name of God, such contradictory conceptions of life and social behaviour, then something very serious is happening to the content of this key term, "God." Either this is such a general and abstract term that it can bear any content we care to project on to it in accordance with our position and prejudices, or there is a tragic misunderstanding, vast and far-reaching, as to the precise and specific meaning of the word "God."

As long as we approach this major question from the standpoint of historical reference to Jesus Christ, the first alternative is, on principle, untenable. Jesus was not some extra-terrestrial being who came down to preach a "God" so far above human daily life, so removed from social conflicts and history, as to be indifferent or equally close to any human condition, any type of interpersonal behaviour, any social actions, any order established or projected by which people live together. On the contrary, in the highly conflictive world of his time and place, Jesus—as God's witness—took well-defined options and positions, acted against many of the dominant religious and social conventions, risked his life to correct the misunderstandings and distortions underlying these conventions, and—in the end—was condemned and executed for his resultant witness to a God who was the opposite of the "God" of the established socio-political and religious order. Since then, we who believe in Jesus Christ have believed that through his resurrection from the dead, his

God was confirmed as the true one, and that of his judges was shown to be the false one. We believe that in this "crisis," this judgment pronounced by God between Jesus and those who condemned him (see John 8:37–55; 16:8–15), we have been given the definitive key—operable at any time, in any social and ecclesiastical situation—for recognizing the true image of the living God, as distinct from caricatures and falsifications.

This, then, is not a question of interest only to academic theology: it is a matter of life or death for our Christian faith; in the short term, it can be literally a matter of life or death for men and women, since these days—like in those of Jesus and the early church—we can be called to give up our very lives in the name of God, while others can plan the deaths of those who resist their orders, "thinking thereby to serve God." Can this giving up of life be "in vain," can these lives be "lost"? Or do those who plan deaths deserve to have Jesus' words applied to them: "They will do this because they have not known the Father or me" (John 16:3)?

5. IF GOD EXISTS, WHICH IS THE TRUE GOD?

Given this situation, the main question for us is not so much whether God exists, but which is the true God. That is, our "God problem" is not so much atheism, but idolatry. So we need to ask not just if God exists, but what God is it that exists: how this one can be recognized and known, what this one does in our lives and our history, and how we, given our basic attitudes and present behaviour, can correspond, personally and collectively, to this God.

(From this it follows that, in Latin America, the "christological question" is not so much whether Jesus is or is not the Son of God, as what God he is Son of and what he was like in his actual life on earth. Also, where most people are Catholic, the "church problem" is not so much whether or not the church has to be devoted entirely to the service of God, as which God it must serve and what actual form this service must take if it is to show forth this God. And finally, where the majority of the people are "believing and oppressed," the important thing is not to go on saying that "human liberation" is clarified and finally achieved only in relation to God, but which God human beings are made in the image of, and how this God acts in history to set human beings free, which God we have to meet in order to achieve fullness of life, personal and collective.)[13]

In deciding our basic "God problem," we see ourselves as being closer to the religious problematic of the people of the Bible than to the secularized societies of the First World, or to the way in which European and North American theology has interpreted this problematic and tried to reply to it.

In the Bible, in effect, there is no perceived alternative between belief and non-belief, in the modern sense. The great "God problem" that keeps reappearing there is always posed within religious "belief"; the problem is a challenge and temptation not to atheism, but to idolatry. And in the Bible, this problem is not so much—as we "educated" classes tend to think—that of superstition and the primitive religiosity of the "simple" people, who see God in relation to their basic needs. No, the problem is rather the "idolatry" of the privileged, "cultured" groups, who use God more or less deliberately to legitimize their piled-up wealth, their exclusive knowledge, their power to dominate; it is the "atheism" of the ruling groups, who believe God will not see their exploitation of the people and murder of innocents, will not hear the cries of the oppressed.[14]

In Europe and North America, the subject of God has been brought up to date in recent decades mainly for the purposes of dialogue with atheistic humanism in its various guises.[15] On the "Christian continent" of Latin America, on the other hand, with its "believing and oppressed" masses, the same subject has become urgent and in need of renewal for the sake of active resistance and liberating witness in the face of anti-human idolatry.

This is not to say that secularization and non-belief are not problems in Latin America too, in an increasingly homogeneous cultural world. There is a new culture spreading into the majorities in most regions—more urban and technological, and above all more political.[16] And this spread, most noticeably among the younger generation, brings a crisis of traditional religious beliefs, a crisis of "God." But this crisis is generally that of a certain received image of God, including that of idols who, usurping

God's holy name, have often taken the place of the living and
true God in our "Christian civilization." So the main question
for our theology and our evangelizing witness as church is not
so much whether we are believers or atheists, as which God we
are believers in or atheists toward. The early Christians, let us
not forget, were also called "atheists" because they did not share
current beliefs or accept the religion of the Roman Empire.[17]

This, then, is the prime concern of this volume. It has a double motivation: First, a negative one, to criticize the commonly
held images and caricatures of God current in our society and
often among us Christians and pastoral workers; more radically,
to unmask falsifications of God, denouncing the idols that foster
the domination, marginalization and death of the poor.[18] Second, the volume has a positive motivation: to contribute to a
search for the living face of God, for God's liberating presence
among the poor, for the way God moves in our midst; to proclaim the surprising novelty of the true God, the God of humble
service, joyous solidarity and life in abundance for all God's
children. Some readers — especially priests — whose education
took place some while back, will find that this approach to "the
God of Christians" is a blank in the theological training they
received. It is not exactly what we studied under *De Deo uno,* a
treatise that certainly referred to scripture but whose concerns
and methodology corresponded more to a philosophical
approach: to the "existence" and "attributes" of a God accessible through the "right use of reason." Nor is it quite what we
found under *De Deo trino,* which certainly dealt with God as
revealed in the biblical history leading up to Jesus Christ, but
did so with the overriding concern of achieving the most precise
formulations of the mystery of the one God in a Trinity of persons, and according to a historico-dogmatic methodology: a
methodology concerned with the historical genesis and right
understanding of the dogma of the Trinity in the church. What
we now need, between these two treatises, and using a more
biblical and experiential approach, is a study of how this living
God, finally revealed as the God and Father of Jesus Christ,
whom Jesus showed us and taught us in the Spirit to call "Our
Father," acts personally in relation to us. In biblical terms, this
is the God of Israel (Old Testament), the Father of Jesus Christ

and the God of Christians (New Testament); in terms of the creeds, it is the one God, Father and creator; in trinitarian terms, it is the first person of the Blessed Trinity.

This gap in seminary theology has, naturally, been replicated in preaching and catechesis. Post-Tridentine catechesis generally referred to God as "the infinitely perfect Being, creator of heaven and earth," and to a God who is "unique in a Trinity of persons," one of whom is Jesus Christ as the incarnate Son. But it did not usually speak of the true face of the living God revealed to us as the Father of Jesus Christ, nor of the personal way this living God acts toward us in history. In recent decades, with the biblical and catechetical renewal, there has been a fairly vigorous resurgence of the "subject" and witness of the God of Christians, both in theology and in pastoral practice, starting in Europe and North America, and, with the differences noted above, gaining ground in Latin America in the 1970s.[19]

CHAPTER II

God on Our Journey
in Faith

The foregoing leads to the need to explain more historically and analytically the social and cultural setting in which we seek to do theology: What are the real conditions of the spiritual experience that requires and sustains our theological endeavour? What are the fundamental perspectives, concerns and criteria — more technically, the hermeneutical keys — that guide our interpretation of the basic, permanent texts that contain the Judeo-Christian revelation of God? In order to attempt to answer these questions, this chapter will contain something like a "theology of story," which is perhaps closer to the theological genres of the Bible and the sort of theology being done "on the hoof" in the base communities among the poor, than to the theology that has been current in Western academic circles since the high scholasticism of the Middle Ages. The "story," told here contemplatively and reflectively, cannot encompass the whole of what our believing people have experienced as a totality. Rather it reflects a new process, the most meaningful and renewing process taking place in the light of the biblical tradition itself. In part 2 of this work, this new process will serve as the hermeneutical key for examining the faith and history of a people in more detail.

1. THE CHURCH AND THE POOR IN LATIN AMERICA

I am concerned here with the recent past and the present,
the time since Vatican II, when, as even secular historians recognize, one of the most important events in Latin America has
been the new alliance between the Catholic Church and the
poor, who make up the majority of this dark-skinned continent.
How is this an "event"? Because it really is something new, and
something enormously important both for the peoples of the
continent and for the church. It is not the first time the church
has been concerned with the poor and has worked on their
behalf, but what I believe is new, at least since the late eight-
eenth or early nineteenth centuries, is this close relationship
being built up — not without hitches and confusion — between the
church and the poor mass of the people. I am speaking of the
actual, institutional Catholic Church, as it exists at diocesan and
parish level, with its priests and religious and lay organizations,
the tangible church as a social entity, made up of particular
groups and organizations, each with its own mentality and
dynamic.

For at least a century and a half, this institutional church was
based in non-poor sectors of society. (I say "non-poor" to avoid
giving offence, though the poor, today as in the Gospels, can
talk without bitterness of "the rich," those who do not live and
are not "like us." I know it is not a sociologically precise term,
but it corresponds, from the viewpoint of the poor, to a real and
very deep experience.) Seen from the perspective of the poor,
the church was based (and still is, in part) in another world,
among other people: those who appear on television, those the
commercials are addressed to because they have the money to
buy things, those for whom the laws are made and for whom the
government governs, those who are educated and make proc-
lamations, those who have the wealth, the word and the power
in these lands. "The church is over there; that's where its centre
is; that's where it comes to us from. It brings us good things:
powdered milk, the sacraments, the catechism. The priests come
from over there, bringing their teaching and their ceremonies,
their way of speaking and their customs; when they come to us,

they make their houses like those over there." It is a church that at times still "comes" to the poor, "missionizing" them from outside. That, however, is changing, and recent years have seen something quite new: a new relationship building up between the church and the real poor, the masses of the people. The church, or at least part of it, has moved to the poor.

Many church people, persons who are part of church institutions, have sought to make their dwelling among the poor, to "become incarnate" in the people. In one family in my working-class "township" in Santiago, they said to me: "See, skinny, we've got you tied down here now." Meaning: "You're not a visitor here anymore; we can count on you; you're one of us now." That does not mean that we priests and sisters who come from outside are no longer privileged; we are — through our education, our contacts, our securities. Personally, I have never felt my privileged position so acutely as now, after twelve years of living among the poor. I don't fool myself into thinking I have become one of them. To a certain extent, however, thanks to their welcome, their openness in sharing what they have with those they feel have come to serve them, I do feel part of their world. And we have learned a lot from the world of the poor: we have assimilated part of their culture and their values; we have learned to look at society through their eyes, to see life and death, living together and celebrating, poverty itself and deprivation, as they do. We have learned much about their faith and hope. All this is what my friends meant by saying they had me "tied down."

Such a movement supposes a real convulsion within the church, affecting the language it generally uses and its mentality: a convulsion that has not taken place in a day, or without difficulties, estrangements and conflicts. But it is perhaps one of the deepest dimensions of what is called "the church's option for the poor." It supposes that the church "opts" for the poor because it has the possibility of so opting: because it is still not the church of the poor, in the sense that the church in Chile is the Chilean church, with no possibility of opting not to be so. The church needs to opt for the poor because it still has to go to the poor: here is the church, there are the poor, and it has to move from one place to the other. This involves making a conscious choice, which means revising our mental categories, our view of things, behaviour, way of life and surroundings.[1] Above all, it means revising our understanding of the gospel and faith, which can change in surprising ways when viewed from the situation, experience and viewpoint of the poor.

This brings in another formula, another expression pregnant with meaning, which completes the picture of this new church-poor relationship. The "option for the poor" describes a movement that starts with the church. But there is also the inverse and corresponding movement, which we call "the irruption of the poor into the church." As church "agents" move to the poor, live with them and open our doors to them, so the poor come in, pile in, and begin to fill the seats and speak, so that the church itself begins to take on another tone, to speak in a different way.[2]

Of course, since the beginnings of Christianity in Latin America in the sixteenth century, the church has always been concerned with the indigenous and mestizo majorities, has had the poor inside it. But in that church, in that colonial "Christian society," the poor were a passive, dependent majority that was oppressed by the colonial system; they were taught, given the sacraments and cared for pastorally from above by the church. Or indeed the church abandoned them to their fate in huge areas where missions hardly penetrated; they were "marginal" in relation to the ecclesiastical and colonial centres, just as in more recent times they have been marginalized into huge areas on the periphery of the urban centres where decent folk live and work, where the churches and convents and other church establishments are.[3] Now, by contrast, the poor are taking an active role, making themselves the protagonists of the church. And so this church is increasingly becoming based in the world of the poor and reflecting their concerns: unemployment and insecurity, hunger and fear, solidarity, simple faith and sure hope. The church itself is beginning to look at collective life and society as a whole "with the eyes of the poor," and to act accordingly. As a result, it is beginning to suffer the fate of the poor: to be despised, defamed and persecuted by those who have well-being, formal education and power.

The church opts for the poor and the poor invade the church, taking it over as their house, changing it to their way of life. They are not doing it violence; they are simply realizing what it should always have been, in the logic of the gospel: the church of the poor, follower of Jesus among the poor, demonstrating a God whose will is the liberation of humankind in all dimensions of personal and community life. The poor are taking over the church as something that belongs to them, something that — since the Gospels — should always have been theirs. And so, through two reciprocal movements conditioning one another, each inexplicable without the other, a new relationship between the church and the poor is being forged, an event that has to be seen as one of the most important elements in the history, not just of the church in Latin America, but of Latin America itself in the past few decades.[4]

2. CONVERGENCE: CHURCH, POPULAR CULTURE, POPULAR MOVEMENT

This actual, tangible church, with its personnel and organizations, has moved toward, is taking root and growing in the world of the people. Not only is it working for the poor and with them; it has, at least in part, shifted its axis to them. The poor majorities are not just an amorphous mass of unfortunates; they make up a "world," a people's culture with its own experience of life, qualitatively different from that of us "citizens" of the Western (or "bourgeois") world. My personal experience, from having travelled throughout Latin America and spent years studying in Europe, is that there is far more in common between the middle- and upper-class culture of Santiago and that of Rome, Paris or Munich, than there is between this culture and that of the barrio I live in now. Linguistic problems aside, the differences in overall culture, in the manner of being human and living together, in the values assigned to patterns of life and work, and a host of other things, make a middle-class Chilean feel far more at home in a European city than in one of the fringe townships that make up "Greater Santiago." And the same would be true of all the great cities of Latin America. We are more ignorant of the culture of our townships than we are of European culture.

The double movement of the church to the poor and the poor to the church has brought about a significant convergence between the real church, sociologically speaking, and popular culture. Popular culture here includes a very basic aspect: religiosity or popular piety, the form in which the people experience God and live the Christian faith, the way they live together and share things in their daily lives, thereby intuitively perceiving the gift and demands of that faith.[5] This convergence has modified both the church and, slowly, popular culture. There is a new popular culture, fairly inarticulate, influenced by a number of factors of varying worth, particularly the mass media. And there is a new popular Christianity, being forged in those real laboratories of human culture and renewed faith, the Christian base communities. In them there is a real exchange of influences, in which the people transmit values to us and teach us, the "agents" who come from outside; and we too, while letting ourselves be taught, also transmit values, with greater or lesser success. The people themselves, through coming and bonding together in communities, learn to share, to grow together, and act in solidarity, in new ways. They are an effervescent mass, in which new human beings are slowly taking shape. It is not hard to see men and women of the people who have experienced the renewed church in their area behaving in new ways, thinking and feeling differently. This does not mean that they begin to think and feel like people in the wealthy areas, but that they begin to experience their life as individuals and as a people as dimensions of their Christian faith and human experience.[6]

The church and popular culture are two poles; the convergence process also has a third, forming a triangle of mutual influences with the other two: this is the pole of organizations existing among the people, the popular movement. We speak of a "popular movement of liberation"; this would include the whole history of workers' movements, the trade union movement, people's political parties—with all their ambiguities— insofar as they are truly popular or have taken root in the people, neighbourhood groups, such as youth centres, mothers' centres, and newer types dedicated to claims for basic rights or cultural resistance. All these represent a long tradition of organizing, sharing, struggling together for dignity and less inhuman living conditions. They constitute a whole apprenticeship in human dignity, for women who hold families together, for workers; a means of growth for young people, who can see themselves as part of a people that has to wake up and stand up, win its rights and progress together.[7]

This popular movement, in most of Latin America, has generally developed outside the Christian church, not removed from any Christian inspiration, but away from official church bodies. Till about fifteen years ago, Socialist and Communist parties were generally regarded as enemy organizations in church circles, and trade unions as dangerously ambiguous. Going back a few decades, the workers' movement, for example, was being denounced in clerical discourse as downright demoniacal. Behind this lay a perception—still strong in certain Catholic circles—of the popular movement as an avalanche of hate, a barbarous wave of revenge and violence. Not long ago, I came across a preachers' guide, written by an eminent ecclesiastic and published in Santiago around 1925. It contained an appendix on "the social question," which stated that the root of all social problems was "the envy of the poor." A little strong, perhaps? Not that there is no envy among the poor, and aggression, more often: the poor are human beings and as subject to sin as any others; they also live in a situation that breeds exasperation. More: their world and culture are torn apart and degraded by the dominant culture. But a statement like this, in a guide for preachers, shows how far the institutional church uncritically shared the outlook of the privileged classes. Not surprisingly, this meant that the leaders of the popular movement were generally anti-clerical. If the church was on the side of the rich and the priests friends of the bosses, what else would they be?[8]

So the church has now drawn closer not only to popular culture, but also to the popular movement. Speaking personally, in my "township" I have found that the people have their own forms of organization, and that the people's memory transmits a whole history of suffering and struggle, and of reflection on this struggle. There is a history of the people that has not been written, at least not in the books we studied at school, which were full of conquistadors, presidents, battles and generals. The other history is that of the indigenous peoples, the Mapuches,

who saw the *huincas,* as they called the white colonizers, seize
their lands through deceit and violence; of the peasants, marginalized by the landowners for centuries; of the workers,
exploited and so often bloodily repressed. . . .⁹ This history lives
on in people's consciousness, usually not as written history, but
as oral tradition, as when my grandmother, who came from peasant stock and could hardly read or write, called me to her sick-
bed in 1973 to tell me what she had gone through in the outskirts
of Valparaiso during the civil war of 1891. Ill though she was,
and almost blind, she still had ringing in her ears the echoes of
the hatred and the bloody revenge exacted by "the rich" against
any organization and achievement by the poor. Eighty-two years
later, remembering what had happened then, she thought it
would stand me in good stead in dealing with the effects of the
Pinochet coup, since she remembered how much it had helped
her in 1891 to hear her grandmother telling her about what she
had been through in the wars of independence! The whole span
of Chilean independence, remembered by two virtually illiterate
old ladies! So this is not the history learned from books; it is
the history people have lived through and passed on with the
memory and wisdom of the people, the history of the collective
suffering and struggles of the downtrodden, the memory of
which helps them to go on living and struggling.

Now the church is drawing close to this living history of suffering, exploitation, repression and struggle. We hear about the
Vicariate for Pastoral Care of Workers, we know that the Vicariate of Solidarity defends popular leaders who are persecuted;
we hear that the cardinal has backed the striking miners. . . . All
this has become more or less normal. But it was not normal
twenty-five years ago, much less fifty years ago. Now we hear
our bishops speaking of workers' rights, denouncing unjust laws.
We have the Medellín and Puebla documents, which speak of
"institutionalized violence," of the "cause of the poor," and of
"liberating evangelization." In the base communities, companions are encouraged to engage in local organizations, in trade
unions, to take their Christian witness into the political struggle.
This has become something quite normal—as it has for leaders
of the workers' organizations, even those who are declared
Marxists, to come to the church if they need to meet somewhere

without being overheard, or if they need support in defending someone's rights. Or for joint action to be taken, with the parish priest joining in as one more member. Such things have become quite normal—which does not mean that problems cannot arise, or that we can dispense with critical clarity and a constant search to be true to the demands of the gospel. But the church is in the people's struggle, in its way, as church, and it is encouraging its members, as members too of the people, to commit themselves to the people's struggles for dignity and their rights.[10]

So the church is coming together with popular culture and the popular movement; we now need to look at the third side of the triangle: the convergence between the popular movement and popular piety. The leaders of the people's movement, whether political or trade union, have often all too easily dismissed popular religious feelings and expressions as alienation, "opium." Now they are beginning, through their contact with the base communities, to find that traditional faith has a wide potential for enhancing human dignity and advancing collective liberation; that it forms a basis for a deeper and broader hope, something that can extend beyond the repeated failures of the popular movement.[11] Early in 1974, I had to take part in the funeral of a young militant who had been tortured to death. His companions were totally disconsolate. We sang Psalm 126: "A man goes his way and sows seed with tears. Back he comes, singing, sheaves on his shoulder." On the way back, one of the young men clung to me in tears, saying: "We thought our cause was just." With the people's faith and hope, I was able to answer: "Our cause is just." This—I was told later—made a deep impression on them. The depth of Christian faith and hope is being discovered by many "atheists," many leaders of popular movements who have inherited an anti-clerical, and sometimes anti-religious, tradition.

From another aspect, many of the simpler people, most traditional in faith and culture, are beginning to overcome their prejudices in the base communities, to discover all that is valuable and necessary in the popular movement. They are beginning to hear the Christian call and responsibility to commit oneself to the collective struggle: perhaps in political or trade

union activity, more usually in the network of social organizations growing up in the townships.

3. THE BASIC SPIRITUAL EXPERIENCE

Many historical and cultural factors, some traditional, others
new, are at work in bringing about this convergence between
the church, the popular culture and the popular movement. But
I do not believe that the convergence of these elements would
produce a new human and Christian synthesis without a basic
new human experience "happening" among us, and among the
poor masses all over Latin America, an experience capable of
radically transforming and giving meaning to the whole of
human personal and collective life. This can be called a "spiritual" experience—in the anthropological sense—because it
affects and transforms human beings from their deepest root,
which we call their "spirit," and also because we see in it, in the
light of faith, the transforming and re-founding action of the
Spirit of Jesus Christ, at this privileged time in the history of
our believing and oppressed peoples.

Before analyzing this experience from a specifically believing
viewpoint, however, it might be fruitful to consider it simply as
a basic human experience. Before speaking of a "new collective
experience of God in history," we can—with Vatican II—speak
of a "new humanism, one in which man is defined first of all by
his responsibility toward his brothers and toward history" (GS
55). This radical experience is common to believers and non-
believers alike, and once we have had it, it marks our lives forever. At the same time and for the same reason, it also
differentiates us quite sharply from other Christians who have
not had it—to the point where we can, perhaps mistakenly, come
to think ourselves further removed from such Christians than
from non-believers who share our experience. (In any case—
leaving aside anthropological or cultural differences—our Christian faith tells us that God judges not between believers and
atheists, but between those who open up to love and justice in
their dealings with others, and those who close themselves to
others, concerned only with their own satisfaction and security.
The former really meet God and live in God's grace, even if

they do not accept God intellectually; the latter, even if they accept and offer public worship to God, have in fact not met God.[12] This raises the question: If this is the case, why do we have profession of faith, a community of believers, evangelization and the sacraments? This is not the place to answer this question with the detailed consideration it requires. All I can say here is that such things — along with the church itself — are effectively necessary: not because they are the only and automatic way for each of us to find God's salvation and grace, but rather because humankind needs, and God wills, God's liberating grace to become accepted recognition, a visible body, and a social force in history.)

The radical experience referred to is a whole in life, but has various dimensions which need to be described here. The first is what I would call ethical indignation in the face of the massive impoverishment experienced by the poor and the injustice this represents. By impoverishment and injustice I mean the innumerable, habitual acts of repression and flagrant assault on human dignity, the dignity of individuals and of the people as a whole: kidnapping and assassination of popular leaders; threats and terror sown among settlers and workers; inhuman working conditions; exploitation verging sometimes on slavery. . . . And I am also referring to the long-term, tremendous deterioration of the quality of life for the mass of the people, throughout Latin America: something that is now hardly remarked on — that the people have less to eat, that families are more often broken up, that there is a real epidemic of neurosis, brought on by people not knowing where the next meal is coming from, by so much frustration and bitterness, by young people being systematically denied any meaningful future while every day being shown (even in colour, because you can get that on credit) images of a world full of easy and deceitful happiness. I was talking about this recently to a sister from a neighbouring township. She told me that in her barrio, 80 percent of heads of household were out of work. Many had had the water cut off; most were "stuck" for the money to pay for electricity, using wood stoves to heat water, into which they put a little sugar to stave off the children's hunger. The electricity company was in any case enforcing longer and longer power cuts, and had just cut the power for three whole days. In winter, people started to go to bed at six in the evening, so as to spend fewer hours of hunger, darkness, emptiness: this is the day getting shorter, life itself going out. What is happening in one place is happening—to a greater or lesser extent—all over Chile, all over Latin America.

Seeing all this, and at the same time knowing how other people live and spend, how the material resources of one's country have been squandered, how the whole economy of one's country—and of the whole "Western Christian" world—has been geared to the interests and profit of a minority . . . produce radical indignation. If we know all this and don't feel this indignation, we have no right to call ourselves human beings. We simply cannot remain indifferent to all this, see it as something of secondary or marginal importance in human life; once we know all this, we cannot go back to eating and sleeping, chatting and working, planning and pursuing our own lives in the same way as before. I don't mean that all enjoyment has to go out of our lives, but it has to be a different sort of enjoyment, or we have to earn the right to it in a different way. Once we have found all this, we cannot turn our backs on it without denying ourselves, abdicating our dignity as human beings.[13]

Together with this radical indignation (and in an apparent contradiction that breaks our logical scheme of things), goes the radical astonishment produced by the real miracle of human survival and solidarity. If one tries to tot up family expenditure, knowing their income, on even basic foodstuffs, one can only marvel at how they survive. And not only do they survive: they go on making jokes, laughing and singing—leading a human life, that is. How can they share what they haven't got? How can one woman take in the children of a neighbour who is in hospital? How can a worker risk his job to speak up for his companions? How can the unemployed and others in barrios like the one described above get up to such amazing things? They collect old planks and all sorts of rubbish and light bonfires on the street corners, not only when a protest has been called, but every evening. And the neighbours gather round, warm themselves a little, tell jokes and sing, discuss the situation, make up poems and even put on little plays. That is, they open up a space of human life and creativity. How can they do it, living in such conditions?

It can only be called a miracle. How can the poor keep their faith and hope so alive and fresh, in such an ocean of deprivation, suffering and cruelty as would embitter all human relationships for the rest of us and "scandalize" our faith in God? For many of them, human solidarity is clearly a sign that God is near, as never before. They know that God is the God of the poor, the God who raises up the downtrodden and teaches us to share with others. And they can teach this without sermons: they show it in their behaviour, their reactions, their spontaneous expressions. So all this, this unbelievable resistance in the face of such forces of corruption and death-dealing, these marvellous seeds of new life, can produce only a radical astonishment.

The third dimension of this experience is that of inescapable demand: we cannot pursue a human life if we turn our backs on such a reality. Whatever socio-economic level we belong to, our lives can have no humanly valid meaning if our successes, personal and family achievements, well-being and security — however modest — are built at the price of ignoring this reality, and even of failing to accept our complicity in the causes of so much deprivation and such cruelty. If we do this, all we devote to ourselves is a lie, rotten at the root. Even recognizing that we can break away only partially and slowly from the unjust system that envelops us, we need now to seek simpler ways of living, ones more in solidarity with the poor; we need to see what we can do, in the medium and long term, to combat the structural injustices that lie at the root of so much deprivation.[14] Or, put more positively: the "astonishment" caused by the people's capacity for faith and solidarity must mobilize the best of our energies to serve those values, to make them the guiding principles of a new society; these "miraculous" seeds of human values, faith and hope must make us put our lives at the service of these life currents, this dynamism of resurrection and Reign of God in our history.

4. LIBERATION THEOLOGY

One has to be very careful using this heading, as "liberation theology" has become like a red rag to a bull in the ideological war being waged from the power centres in Latin America. Nor would I want to claim that liberation theology has achieved such a balance that it is no longer in need of refinement, or even of correction. But I should like to explain what many church people, many members of the Christian people, mean when they use the term.

Effectively, it concerns the experience I described in the last section, this basic human experience, now understood in the light of the gospel, in the light of explicit Christian faith, in reference to Jesus Christ and the God of Jesus Christ. This experience can be, and is, common to both Christians and non-believers. Christians, however, have an interpretation of this experience, a referent that allows us to see its coherence, its deepest roots and its transcendent projection. This means that we – Christians in the church – placed in this new situation, feeling this ethical indignation at the unjust destitution of the majority of the people, this astonishment at their powers of survival and the inescapable demands this situation makes on us, begin to have a new experience of God, begin to "understand" God in a new way. And so we speak of "theo-logy," of reflection and discourse on God.[15]

This God is not the "God of the philosophers," the God whom so many experiences and different religions lead to. This is, quite specifically, the God of the people of Israel: the God who called Abraham, who summoned Moses to liberate the Semite clans enslaved in Egypt, who spoke to the people through the prophets, who inspired the prayers of the Psalmists. This is, even more specifically, the God of "the founder of our faith . . . who will bring it to completion" (Heb. 12:2), Jesus of Nazareth; the God whom he called, familiarly, "Abba, Father." This is the God who fortified the faith of Jesus' disciples, who raised the crucified Jesus from among the dead, and who, through him, gives us courage in the Spirit. Now – as was said in chapter I – we meet this God above all in history, not in the history written in books, but in the history we live as a people, in the history of all human struggles for a world with less poverty and injustice; we meet this God through these contradictions: exploitation and solidarity, division and communion, frustration and hope. The whole of this history, which we both undergo and construct, is the main setting for our meeting with the living God.

Using the term "history" emphasizes the collective dimension. The subject of history is actually a people or group of peoples. A "people" is of course made up of individuals and groups, but it is still a people. And in this collective history, we experience this God from the underside, from the side of the oppressed and marginalized, not from the side of conquerors, the ruling classes and the privileged. The substance of the biblical experience of God—in both Old and New Testaments—is that of a revelation taking place in history and from its underside: from the sufferings, resistance and hope of the poor. This experience is witnessed from there, and the message of this God is carried from there to others. For the poor themselves, this message is first the good news of their liberation, but also a demand for conversion and commitment in solidarity. For the others, it is first a demand for conversion, for a break with their old ways, but also and above all an announcement of new life and a genuine way of living together. It is the challenge of this ethical indignation, the witness of this radical astonishment, and the call of this inescapable demand for commitment, for a change of lifestyle, for placing one's very life at the service of the poor: a challenge and a witness from the living God, through the prophetic and lifegiving Spirit.

This same basic content can also be found in the inverse, or rather correlative and convergent, movement. This is the experience discovered along the way by many men and women "of good will" who are non-believing fighters for justice, or who at least start out from a position of non-belief. The experience they have—probably without reflecting on it—is that this underside of history contains a demand for justice and human dignification that precedes them and against which they have to measure their whole lives; that there is a horizon of hope extending beyond all calculation and all the frustrations that history can throw into their paths. More radically—or perhaps more precisely—it is the experience of a call, a strength, a presence, a life-force and source of life exceeding all conditions of life. In conjunction with committed and explicit Christian witness, this presence can be recognized as that of the God of the poor, of justice on behalf of the oppressed (ethical indignation); as the liberating God, who works marvels and is seen giving life and strength to the weak (radical astonishment); as the holy and demanding God, questioning us radically, but also setting us free, if we allow ourselves to be led by the Spirit and respond with the whole of our lives (inescapable demand): in short, as the God of the Kingdom proclaimed by the prophet of Nazareth, as the God and Father of Jesus Christ himself.

So it is "liberation theology": because we meet the living and true God in history, in the history of the poor and their liberation; or because this history of the liberation of the poor brings us face to face with the God of Jesus Christ. Whichever way we approach it, it is the basic "spiritual experience" that we need to make the object of our reflection.[16]

5. A HISTORICAL READING OF THE GOSPEL

What lines should our reflection follow? How can we set about defining this experience? How can we set about constructing a new Christian language on the basis of it? The answer to all these questions is: through a historical reading of the gospel.

Something new is happening in the church communities among the poor in Latin America: the people are taking the gospel into their own hands. They are no longer hearing just a few teachings and some miracle stories of the Jesus Christ of the Gospels, more or less accurately interpreted by preachers. Now, with the Gospels in their hand, standing shoulder-to-shoulder and with their feet firmly planted on the ground, they are discovering that Jesus was "one of us": a flesh and blood human being, poor of the poor, living in circumstances similar to theirs; a man of the people, who had to make choices and take risks in a history like theirs. They are discovering the teacher with a very specific message for the simple people of his time in Palestine and for our times in our countries: a teacher who was not a doctor of law or a priest of the Temple, just a simple popular preacher who understood the soul of his people, shared their fate and spoke to them from within their experience of poverty and rebuttal, from within their religious tradition and their hope — and who from there bore witness to the tenderness of the Father, to the liberating power of the Kingdom to come, already being brought in by him. They are discovering Jesus' "style," the way he lived and related to people, his specific gestures and his practice, his strategy of liberation: all of which are as pregnant with meaning for them as his words, and inseparable from these (see DV 4).

From the standpoint of Jesus' actual history and the choices he made within it, in that particular society and in the face of the powers that ruled it, the people now are also discovering the roots and import of Jesus' destiny: of his death and resurrection. Maligned and persecuted, arrested at night and tortured, put on show as a subversive and blasphemer, condemned at a false trial and executed . . . and all for reasons of "national security," or, more especially, for having questioned the dominant religious practices and concepts. These things were done to him because his practice of bringing life and liberation to those at the bottom of society subverted the order and legality of those at the top, and because his witness to the God of the poor, the uneducated, the public sinners, radically called into question the "God" of the rich, the learned, and the pious. But beyond the suffering and derision of the cross, beyond the bitter frustration, fear and dispersion of the disciples . . ., God raised up God's servant Jesus, confirmed the testimony of the Son, finally consecrated the Messiah of the poor, and carried on his work through the outpouring of the Spirit on his followers: the Spirit of life and freedom, of strength and solidarity, of love and hope enduring all things.

The simple people are discovering this human, historical Jesus against the backdrop of their deep faith in the Christ, the Son of God, God like the Father. They are rediscovering with joy that this Son of God became "one of us," became poor among the poor, became one of the oppressed people. This discovery is a radically liberating experience for them. They — those who have always been shoved aside, put to the back of the queue — now know with a new realism that "it is not like that with God," because their God is the God of Jesus, and Jesus himself is "God with us." The people are rediscovering this real Jesus, this Messiah of the poor, who, with such human gestures and with so much freedom, showed the face of a God who is Father/Mother, no longer the Great Dictator of the universe, not a God who punishes, but one who is full of tenderness and friendship, the God of life and hope, the God of the Spirit: hope of the poor, strength of the weak, joy of the persecuted.[17]

Also, the people are discovering, through their own communities and reading the New Testament, the image of the early Christian community, the communities of the risen Lord, brought together and animated by the Spirit of Christ. They are finding out that these were communities of poor people, slaves, uneducated people, "just like us": communities living off their recent experience of Jesus and their simple solidarity, shown in sharing bread and wine, the ordinary everyday food: "tea and biscuits," as it were; communities whose mission was to give inescapable witness in favour of the life and rights of the poor, and who for that very reason were attacked and persecuted just as Jesus was; communities that did not live in idyllic harmony, but were threatened by meanness and torn by conflict, internal to each or in relation to other units of the wider church.[18] The people are discovering all this with joy, and feeling more than ever that they are church, the same church they learn about from the New Testament, a church which also had its tensions and conflicts, but had, too, the Spirit of the risen Lord, just as the church of the people has now, a Spirit that is an invincible force.[19]

6. GOD OF THE POOR, GOD OF THE CHURCH

The people are finding a deep similarity between their own church communities and the early communities described in the Gospels and the Acts of the Apostles: communities which bore witness to the God of Jesus, the Christ, in their Jewish world, torn between the age-old passivity of the marginalized and an exacerbated apocalyptic messianism; communities which often bore this witness in the strong sense of "martyrdom" in the face of the weight and threats of a formalistic religion in league with the occupying power. They also recognize the little churches that spread through the Greco-Roman world, as described in the same Acts, in the Letters of St Paul and other writings of the New Testament: communities of weak and despised people, which, surrounded by the pomp and prestige of a fascinating civilization and idolatry, proclaimed the God who raised a crucified Jew; threatened and "martyr" communities faced with the great power of an empire aspiring to monolithic unity—political and religious—and using its "anti-subversive" laws and strategies to this end.

In this way, the church in Latin America, through the base communities of the simple people, is on the one hand rediscovering the God of history, liberator of the oppressed; on the other, it is rediscovering, in the persons of the poor, the God of the original gospel witness, the God of the church. Our church, by rooting itself in the humble people, is coming to recognize its own God in the God of the poor; at the same time, the poor, an oppressed and believing people, as they organize themselves in communities and break into the ecclesiastical institution, are recognizing their own God in the God of the church.[20]

This is the theological (or theologal) nucleus of this reencounter and new alliance taking place between the church and the poor of Latin America. It can be formulated, as the Puebla Final Document does, in christological terms: on one side, the institutional church (speaking through the bishops) is finding that in the "very concrete faces" of the poor and oppressed of the continent, it recognizes "the suffering features of Christ the Lord, who questions and challenges us" and sets us free (Puebla 31–9); on the other, the simple people of the peripheries of the cities and the countryside are finding that they can recognize, in a church that has drawn closer to them and become more of a servant church, and in their own new experience of base church communities, the Christ of solidarity and service, who sets them free and commits them to their own liberation (see Puebla 623–24, 629, 640–43). This is one way of expressing the same nucleus of this reencounter between the church and the poor, which enables us to witness that: "Jesus Christ, living in his church and particularly among the poorest, wishes today to exalt the likeness of God in his people" (Puebla 330).

It is the task of the present work to investigate this nucleus, in the light of the word of the Bible and the tradition of the church, while at the same time examining the Bible and the tradition of the church in the light of this living nucleus of experience of the living God in our midst. We live this experience, understand it and need to deepen it "in a biblical key" — in the perspective of God's self-revelation fulfilled once and for all in the history of Israel, the Christ event and Christ's first witnesses. But, in turn, we need to read and examine these biblical texts not haphazardly, but with reference to this same nucleus of experience of the living God among us: from the standpoint of our poor people awakening to their liberation, from that of the believing communities of the poor on their way to liberation, communities that are becoming the setting for the poor's experience of universal ecclesial communion (Catholic and/or ecumenical).

The two basic criteria or interpretative keys that guide us to read the Bible as God's living word and self-revelation — the church communion and the liberation of the oppressed — spring from this living nucleus, in which we recognize the God of the poor and the God of the church. (Any texts, particularly those from a distant historical and cultural setting, like those of the Bible, need to be "interpreted" or "translated" [Greek *hermeneutica*] for the culture and situation of the community reading them if they are to be understood and transmit their message. To be faithful to the text, this interpretation has to respect its original meaning and place itself in the current of its living tradition. These are the conditions observed in practice by the [explicit or implicit] application of "criteria" or "principles" of interpretation. With biblical texts, the original meaning is framed in the overall meaning of the Bible as a dynamic whole, and the living tradition is provided by the church communion of a believing people. Both are subject to the action of the same Spirit.) So we have two "hermeneutical principles" which, in coherence with the good news of the Kingdom and the following of Jesus Christ that make up the core of the Bible, are inseparable and correlative: what the church believes and experiences, leading to the historically verifiable liberation of the oppressed; and what serves the human liberation of our oppressed people, enlightened in all its depth and transcendental import by the faith and witness of the church.[21]

PART TWO

GOD SEEN FROM OUR SITUATION

INTRODUCTION

Cultural Processes and the Christian Experience of God

Parts 2 and 3 aim to provide a dialectical correlation between believing experience and the tradition of faith, between our own history with God and the biblical history of God and the people of God which culminates in Jesus Christ. This will enable us better to formulate the underlying meaning of our experience in the light of the tradition of the biblical God, and at the same time it will enable us better to translate the content of that tradition as a living message for us.

There is no easy way to formulate the theo-logical meaning of our situation and the corresponding translation of the biblical revelation of God. There is no spiritual or theological "technique" for producing a definitive answer acceptable to all Christian bodies. For one thing, the tradition of faith in God has not reached us in words fallen from heaven, but through witnesses and formulations that—though in some way "inspired" by God in the people of God—originated in a collective experience and a human quest, conditioned by the circumstances and mentality of very remote times and cultures, and then subject to a long and complex history. All of this makes the content of the "tradition of God" very far from being clear to us from the outset.

Even with the greatest good faith and fidelity to the church, we cannot understand this tradition simply by translating it literally into modern languages and applying it mechanically to new situations and experiences.

For another thing, our own experience and the collective history we are undergoing also come to our understanding full of ambiguities. Even supposing that we have "put ourselves" among the poor majorities and have a practical understanding of the processes of liberation, the same events and processes can be experienced by different groups and individuals in different and even contradictory ways. These divergent experiences and interpretations—of the presence or absence of God in the same history—are affected by a variety of complex and deep-rooted personal and social conditionings. So we have to accept that neither the inner dynamic of our history as oppressed peoples, nor our experience or committed practice of liberation, can of themselves lead our believing people to recognize the action of God there, or to deepen their experience of God in a more Christian direction.

We have to bear in mind that both the Christian tradition of God, including the documents in which it is contained, and the experience of our political and cultural processes, including our analysis of them, are historical entities. This means that both the revelation of God in the Bible and Christian experience of God in our history cannot come to us outside a particular mental and cultural framework, made up of the situation and understanding produced by a period and a social setting, with the influences at work on these, taking account of the courses followed by individuals, groups and historical currents. Hence the need for adequate information about, and careful analysis of, our own experience and historical processes; hence also—as noted earlier—the importance of scrupulous application of "hermeneutical principles" for interpreting biblical texts as a living message for us. In both cases, we need critical and shared discernment, in docility to the same prophetic Spirit who inspired the scriptures and who acts today in the historical processes that bring liberation and life to our peoples.

The Bible—as we shall see in more detail in part 3—is a collection of texts and traditions covering more than a thousand years of history of Israel and early Christianity. This history is disturbed and complex, made up of a variety of processes and currents, not just successive, but also parallel and sometimes conflicting. On top of this, we are separated from the latest New Testament writings by nineteen centuries of history of Christian belief in God, and this is an incomparably more varied and complex history than that of biblical times, reaching out as it does to virtually all corners of the planet and all the human cultures inhabiting it.

It is well here to remind ourselves briefly of the outlines of this history of Christian belief in God, and to note the marks it has left on the image of God and language of faith we have received, and on the religious attitudes and practices we know as "traditional." So, in classical antiquity, there was the translation of the living God of Judeo-Christian history into the concepts of the impassive infinite that were proper to Greek metaphysics, and, more importantly, into the longing for extrabodily and extraworldly salvation typical of the dominant Greco-oriental religious idea, with its ideals of stoic asceticism and Platonic mysticism current among the elites.[1] Then, in the Middle Ages and after, the living God of Judeo-Christian history was transformed into the image of God as father and creator found in Romano-Germanic and Iberian-American colonial Christendom, with his attributes of divine providence and distant judge, demanding expiatory sacrifice and having to be appeased through the mediation of saints. Coming to modern times, there is the one God and supreme authority of the Roman ecclesiastical authority, which defines itself as sole teacher of truth in the face of the fissiparous threats, first from subjective interpretation of the Bible (Protestantism), then from the rationalist emancipation of the bourgeoisie (the Enlightenment, positivism, democracy).[2] Our own times, particularly among the older generation, are still marked by the influence of the "received" catechesis inspired by Tridentine clericalism; this influence has helped shape the "traditional" image of God; our own times are also marked by the traits of the popular image of God, which has influenced a degree of autonomy and ancestral resistance to official preaching about God.[3] Finally, there is the God of post–Vatican II pastoral approaches to the middle classes, with the tension produced in our church today between this "renewed" image of a God of personal harmony and social reconciliation, and the more popular and prophetic image of a God who frees the oppressed and promises life to the poor majorities.[4]

There is no space here to expand on this extremely sketchy history. I prefer to move on to a more spacious analysis of what we see happening today to faith in God and actual experience of this, in and around the base communities of the "popular" milieux. This is the broad setting for the "story" of the believing people on their march that I tried to tell in chapter II. It is the setting for the history and the sub-culture of the oppressed majorities of Latin America, in which—somewhat distortedly— the wider cultural processes spread or induced from the great centres of Western culture and power also act as cross-fertilizing agents.[5]

This cross-fertilization is seen in its most acute and indeed dramatic form in the "sub-world" of popular youth culture, where young people are going through a cultural crisis which involves conflict with their parents and the adult "world" in general. Critical new factors are at work here: some deriving from formal education with its scientific-technological bias, contrasting with the religious-humanities bias of the previous generation; others deriving from political groups and movements with a more historical and combative stance, contrasting with the more cosmic and passive stance of traditional mestizo culture. There are also more personal, affective factors, such as the often intense experiences of friendship and solidarity among the people, leading them to question many of the institutions and customs of established society, many values and practices of their elders. On top of all this, there is the overriding influence of television on the more passive elements among the young, an influence that in general tends simply to domesticate them in the dominant materialism, castrating their more human faculties of critical thinking and bonding in solidarity.[6]

This cultural "twist" represented by the emergence of a new generation with different values, this "generation conflict" with the deep crisis of identity young people feel as they try to find their own identity through discovery of new values, brings with it—as one would expect—a crisis of "God": a crisis of faith or religious belief, a feeling, more or less conscious and critical, of distance or even aversion from the image of God and religious attitudes handed on by the older generation.

Not that the crisis is purely a generational one: a deeper and earlier cause is the process of urbanization and secularization of culture coming to fruition in the new generation. This "secularization," as we saw in part 1, does not share all the characteristics of the process in the so-called "developed" world; it shows rather in a progressive "politicization" of consciousness, social relationships and conduct. So there is a deep and widespread crisis, but it is not a question of a pure and simple break with the world view, basic values and lifestyle traditional to the people. There is rather a dialectic of continuity and break, indicating a hesitant quest and desire for a new cultural synthesis. And where this new synthesis is being worked out within the sphere of or under the influence of the new base church communities, it incorporates Christian faith in God, a faith purified and revitalized by the new "spiritual experience" and historical reading of the gospel described in chapter II.

Part 2 sets out to examine this crisis of "God" in the context of this "twist" in the cultural progress of the people on the way to a new cultural synthesis. Such an examination depends on the work already done by specialists in anthropology and social psychology, and merely takes up the more significant components of the process as they affect the crisis of "God." It does so by following the trail of the main questions humankind always asks about God in relation to its experience of the world and its own human existence. Each of these questions is susceptible of a Christian theo-logical reading: that is, an attempt to discern what it offers by way of purification of our received belief in God, or, more positively, by way of new opportunities to find and proclaim the God of Jesus Christ in our present context. The objective is a more lucid reevangelization of our faith in God, a re-evangelization that, on our collective historical journey, will make that faith at once more personal and more prophetic, thereby recapturing the best believing tradition of the people. So the two following chapters deal with the five main questions, as I see them, each under the following subheads:

(a) cultural process; (b) crisis of "God"; and (c) new perspectives. The first sets out the contrast between old and new in the process; the second notes the image of God or experience of God that produces "crisis" in this context, in that it is more of a stumbling-block than a mediation for perceiving the living God; the third, finally, picks out some elements of biblical faith in God that seem to take on new meaning and actuality in the light of the present crisis, and also shows how many basic features of the traditional faith of the people either retain or recover their validity in these new perspectives.

CHAPTER III

God and the World

1. GOD AND NATURE

(a) Cultural Process

In order to assess the depth of the cultural change that has taken place and is still proceeding in the perception of the relation between God and nature, we need to start by examining the way Latin American peasants lived only a generation or two ago; we need to explore their thought processes and their world view. Then there is what has happened to country people who have more recently moved to the cities, particularly those who have come from the most remote areas, where things have changed little in the last twenty years, unlike in the more "suburban" areas.

In their own "world," country people live tied to the soil and their own place; their days and nights are measured by light and dark; their time is measured by long journeys on foot behind an ox cart, or by broken-down country buses that come once a day and do not move much faster than the ox cart. Their subsistence is dependent not only on their physical labour and bodily health, but also on the quality and fertility of the land, on the heat of the sun and the cycle of rains, and the threat of plant and animal pests. Their own health is dependent on "nature" itself, with its strengths and weaknesses; they live in constant fear of sickness and other "ills," as difficult to control as they are to explain.

This way of life still persists strongly among the older generation living in the "townships" or barrios that have sprung up around the big cities, where they re-create a corner of rural life on a few square yards of land. But the man of the family may have found work in a factory, where he has to get used to other tools, or on a building site, where the materials he deals with are industrial products and he is dealing with more advanced techniques. His wife may shop in the market and chat with neighbours, just like in the village she came from, but she will also go to the supermarket and have become familiar with television and its commercials. Their children will have received secondary education or vocational training, and could be driving a Mercedes truck, could be working at some more technological job, or could, indeed, be unemployed. Such changes involve a whole shift in their way of life, of relating to things, of taking stock of themselves as human beings and looking at their possibilities and limitations. A whole "cultural process" has taken place in the space of two generations, or even one, sometimes involving painful upheavals and difficult demands.

For the older generation there had once been (and in some cases there still is) a very intimate relationship with nature, in which they felt part of the natural world, subject to the cycles and laws it imposed as part of a self-evident reality. Now the younger generation especially are standing back from nature, seeing themselves as independent "agents," not submerged in the world of things, seeing nature as something set out before them, as a quarry providing materials from which to build their world according to their means and needs. Human beings are seen more as responsible agents, and nature more as an object, or conglomerate, subject to use and abuse by human beings. This is a result of the cultural impact of science and technology, learned in school or absorbed unconsciously through daily life in the city: science revealing the secrets of nature and how its processes "function"; technology enabling them to channel nature, fashion it with their hands, organize fragments of nature and use them for the benefit of human beings, or the convenience of certain groups.

Before, nature was something lived from within as a given whole, with its necessary and invariable order and seasons.

There was scarcely any room for thinking that life in and with nature might have been, or might come to be, different in some way. Now, and especially for young people, it is obvious to think of the present state of nature as the result of a long process of evolution, and as a passing phase in a process in which human beings have played an active part and will, for good or evil, play an increasingly active one. We may have once thought that this activity was only for the good, but we have now learned better: we have learned that natural resources and the possibilities for manipulating natural processes are not unlimited, and that nature itself — the environment, our bodies and even our minds — has structures and rhythms that cannot be violated with impunity. This is leading us to appreciate a simpler way of life, more physical and less removed from nature, but we have left the "innocence" and spontaneous dependence on nature of pre-urban cultures irretrievably behind.

(b) Crisis of "God"

This whole process of deep cultural change is bound to bring changes to people's traditional experience of God, or else to remove it altogether. The received manner of perceiving the presence of God, of seeing the influence of God on the world and daily life, is bound to be challenged either to change profoundly, or to be relegated to a marginal corner of life.

Country people, and many older people, spontaneously experience this belonging to the natural world, this dependence on the forces and cycles of nature, with a deep sacral or religious sentiment. The beauty of the world with its order and rhythms, nature as dispenser of the good things of life, are seen as an admirable, marvellous reality. One step back into primitive mentality and nature can be seen to contain sacred, beneficent powers, whose friendship it is wise to cultivate. In both cases — with varying degrees of purity of Christian faith — nature is seen as showing the all-embracing presence of a God who is creator and Lord of the world, source of all life, master and provider of physical life and daily health. The other side of the coin is that when nature turns inhospitable — when children are sick or one's own body becomes burdensome and painful, when unseasonal storms or frosts destroy the crops, when "the situation" keeps on getting worse, when nothing sells and there is no work and nothing to eat—then dependence on nature is experienced as cruel oppression by natural forces and the power of death, as a terrifying world. Again, one step back, and nature is seen to contain powers and "evils" that have to be placated. And in both cases—with more or less Christian clarity—nature shows the presence of the same creator God, Lord and master of our life and death, and even fearful overseer and vengeful judge.

Both the wonderful and the fearful aspects of nature constitute what we call a "mediation" of God. Experience of the world is at the same time, intuitively, religious experience, admiration or fear of God—not as a result of reasoning or reflection: "Of course, God created the world and so is the first cause underlying all this. . . ." The world itself and life dependent on nature are rather experienced spontaneously as a "sacrament" of God, as a manifestation of God's presence and human dependence on God, now and always. This is a basic experience that occurs—as I have observed—in a more or less pure form with respect to Christian faith, since it contains a certain degree of persistence of pagan sacral experience, in its animistic or magical form, whose alienating effects can sometimes be terribly oppressive and destructive of human life and society (see Puebla 308–9).

In the "urbanized" life we lead now, on the other hand, natural objects and processes have acquired a more "objective" sense. They are objects and phenomena, undoubtedly with their own laws, which we cannot always understand or control, but they are there as a challenge to human capability and responsibility. Furthermore, in our daily lives, nature as a great system preceding human beings, as a "given," has been pushed into the background. Our daily world is not that of mountains and trees, sea and sun—God's work—but that of streets and buildings, electric light, vehicles and industrial products—the work of human beings with their industry and technology, all ordered for or against the common good. Our daily surroundings are no longer nature, God's creation and sacrament of God's presence, but the city, work of human hands, reflection of the beings and society that we are. So it is natural that the received image of the God of nature, and previously current forms of experiencing

God in everyday life, should be in fairly generalized crisis.

Our relationship with the world and our everyday lives have brought about a crisis of God as creator and providence. More precisely, there is a crisis of the image of the creator as universal "first cause," fabricator and animator of the world as a finished and unchangeable work; a crisis of the image of providence as universal provider and guide, disposing everything in the world, giving and taking away, directly controlling the elements of the cosmos and human life. We can no longer conceive of God as cosmic watchmaker, making a perfect machine and leaving it to run through the centuries with exact and inexorable precision; nor as cosmic driver, seated at the wheel of the universe, directly responsible for the processes and phenomena of the world and every chance happening in our lives; we can no longer regard ourselves as a mere "object" of God's making, a mere instrument of God's will.

This is not to say that modern urban culture has exhausted our capacity for wonder at nature, or for grasping it as a "sacrament" of God. Their very remoteness can still cause us to wonder at the beauty of ocean or mountain—perhaps more so than those who live by them all their lives. We can savour this wonder as a liberation from the daily grind and duties of urban life, which can often become an oppressive servitude; we can experience it as a genuine (re)encounter with the God of liberty and of life. But the fact of our wonder shows that these are exceptional experiences—they are very different from the daily experiences of "pre-urban" men and women.

Furthermore, we cannot say that our new urban sub-culture, particularly as it affects the young, has removed our consciousness of the limits of human beings and our real dependence on nature. These limits are all too painfully present to our young people in the shape of malnutrition and disease. And the deaths of loved ones, particularly when they die young, can give a deep experience of what Western spiritual tradition calls the "sense of contingency," or, in more religious expression, "of creatureliness." But malnutrition, together with the various frustrations and pathologies that affect our young people, is felt increasingly as the unjust result of the social order. And this—often very deep—sense of the fragility of life is no longer felt to be tied to cycles and accidents of the natural world, as it is in peasant culture.

(c) New Perspectives

As Christians living through this cultural process, with the crisis of "God" it entails, we are called to purify our faith and open ourselves to a new experience of the living God, at once more biblical and more liberating of our lives at the present juncture. As believers, our task is not merely to "survive" this crisis, but to accept it and move beyond it, deepening our Christian experience of God and being converted as a result. More particularly, I believe, this crisis of "God" as first cause and providence is calling us to rediscover certain themes in the biblical tradition of the creator God that take on special relevance in our present situation.

I am thinking specifically of the two creation accounts that open the Book of Genesis. (These come from different traditions and date from widely separated periods: the first, Gen. 1:1–2:4a, is the later, and belongs to the "priestly document," known as P, dating from the period of the Babylonian exile in the sixth century B.C. The second, Genesis 2:4b–3:24, is older and belongs to the "Yahwist document," known as J, dating from the early part of Solomon's reign, in the first part of the tenth century B.C.)

These accounts can impress us through the grandeur of the first and the human qualities of the second, but they still come across as somewhat primitive and markedly "mythological" explanations. Secondary education will usually contrast their "primitive and fantastic religious" vision with the "enlightened and objective scientific" view of the world and its evolution. But a more critical and responsible reading will show that they are not at all primitive: of relatively late date and the products of a long poetic and symbolic literary tradition, they in fact express a fairly mature theology of humankind in the world. And their very concept of God, far from being an expression of "natural" experience of God in the world, actually represents a critical stance with regard to the nature theologies current in the great civilizations of the time, and, in a sense, with regard to all "natural theo-logy."

The people of the Bible were able to make a judgment on traditional nature religion from their own original experience of God in history, on the basis of the actions and character of the God they discovered on their believing journey as a people, in the light of the preaching of the prophets (see Amos 4:13; 5:8; 9:6; Isa. 40:28; Deut. 4:32–40). The God who created the world, who formed humankind, who is the source of life for all peoples, is this intensely personal and sovereignly free God, whom Israel came to know when this God brought "our fathers" out of slavery in Egypt—a land of security and plenty—to lead them wandering through the desert to a life of freedom and responsible service: the same God who had called Abraham, making him move out from the pagan security of his family, to lead him wandering toward the land of the promise.[1]

So, rather than read these biblical "accounts" of creation together with current scientific theories about the origin of the world, we should, if we are to grasp their theo-logical message, read them in counterpoint with the "cosmogonies" (myths of the origin of the world) current in the cultural entourage of ancient Israel. These cosmogonies were taken into the Bible, but with a degree of correction that implies a radical transformation of their primitive theology. In order to find the present relevance of the biblical message concerning God as creator, we need, in my view, to look to the theologically most important of these corrections. This will help us to see how we can overcome the crisis of our experience of God in relation to the natural world. What, specifically, are these corrections? I should like to pick out three as being most germane to our current concern:

1. That the world did not "spring" from God out of necessity, by an inner law of the divine life, like a "great body" growing on God. By the same token, this means that God is not the immanent principle or soul of a necessary world, its intrinsic rationale (pantheism); nor is God the great life force animating the world, whose energies we have to seize for our benefit (nature religions); nor do the world and matter respond to an evil principle, essentially opposed to God and corrupting to the spirit (dualism); nor did God create humankind as "pure spirit,"

offering then to save it from its "degradation" in the world and bodily life (spiritualism).

On the contrary, God, through the sovereign freedom of God's word and love, creates a world distinct from God and essentially good (as explicitly stressed in the first Genesis account, with its repeated refrain of God "blessing" the work of creation and seeing that it was "good" and "very good"). Matter and the world cannot be seen as demonic, since they proceed from the creative love of God, which keeps them in being. But neither can they be seen as divine, since they proceed out of God through God's free decision (by contrast with Babylonian and Egyptian accounts) and since God brings them into separate existence, as distinct "objects" with their own structure and dynamism, and, in the privileged case of human beings, with their own freedom really distinct from and "before" God. So God is not natural, as internal principle and soul of the world; and nature is not divine, as a natural emanation from God. God is God, and allows of no admixture or comparison with the world; and the world is the world, an entity that God wills to be.

2. The majesty of the skies, oceans, mountains; the exuberance of forest and jungle; the devastating power of hurricanes and earthquakes . . . all can be recognized as God's work, as a "witness" to God's grandeur, as a setting in which we can meet with God's mystery; they can never, however, be taken as particular "dwelling places" of God, still less as images of God's being.[2] In the biblical creation accounts, as in the whole biblical tradition, the elements and phenomena of nature are not means to God's self-revelation. If the living God has chosen one aspect of the world in which to come to meet us, it is in human beings, in our likeness, in the midst of our people; it is there that God takes on particular features and dwells. If we are to look for a created "image and likeness" of God, these can be found only in human beings: not as "objects," one more physical configuration among so many in the world, but as "subjects"; hence this image and likeness can be found only in what is most properly and exclusively human: personal consciousness, the capacity to love and commit oneself, freedom (see Gen. 1: 26–30; 2:7–8; 2:15 – 3:5).

Therefore, if it is true that we can conceive of God only in mediate or indirect form, through images and from our own experience, then we have to recognize that the most appropriate images and experiences to evoke the living God are those drawn from our own—personal and community—human reality. So God for us is not so much "greater than the universe," or "mightier than the earthquake," as the most intensely personal and most critical consciousness, the most faithful and fruitful love, the most absolutely free will . . . all these beyond what we can imagine, but on these lines.

To say that human beings have been created "in God's image and likeness" means, then, that we may conceive and speak of God only in the image and likeness of human beings (see below, chapter V, section 3[b]). It means, too, that human beings, by the pure fact of being human, are the only "sacred" entities in the whole of creation. Every person and all persons as a human collectivity constitute the true "temple" in which God is made present and communicated to us as in a "sacrament." In the whole world, only persons because they are human, and people because they make up a human community, possess a dignity and rights that are—and must be recognized as—divine. Hence the ire of the prophets in denouncing—as one and the same sin—idolatry and injustice, the corruption of worship, the exploitation of the poor and the assassination of the weak; and their zeal in defending—as one and the same cause—the rights of the poor and oppressed, and the honour and holiness of God (see, e.g., Amos 8:4ff; Hos. 6:4–6; Jer. 7:2b–15; 22:1–9; Isa. 58:1–10).

Of course, the biblical and Christian completion of this viewpoint is to recognize that this "image and likeness" of God have been complete only in the person of Jesus Christ. He alone can say, in all truth: "Who sees me sees the Father" (John 14:8–11; see 1:18). The basis of Jesus' being and personal mystery is to be "the image of the invisible God," and we are all in effect created in the image of this "true Adam" of God's plan (Col. 1:15–20; see 1 Cor. 15:49), who is the Jesus of the gospel story, who was crucified and raised, who today comes to meet us in the suffering faces of our equals, the poor and oppressed, and who in them is revealed to us, questions and challenges us (Matt. 25:31–46; see Puebla 31–9).

3. Human beings are not one more piece in the jigsaw puzzle of the world, subjected blindly to its inexorable laws and destiny. Our dependence on the benefits and threats of nature cannot be a religious dependence (idolatry); nor can it be passively accepted as the immutable "will of God" (fatalism). On the contrary, God alone is "Lord" of the world and of human life, and God gave human beings "dominion" over the natural world; if this has a "soul," God has placed this "soul" in human beings, calling them to "give names" to things and to "increase . . ., fill the earth and subdue it" (Gen. 1:26–30; 2:19–20). This is a call to intelligent work, to science and technology, to progress in gaining knowledge of the natural world, and to rational use of its resources. It is also, and above all, a call to human ethical responsibility: to exercise this "dominion" intelligently and in solidarity with the other elements in the world, without violating the possibilities of nature, for the common good and the genuine advancement of human life.

This is not an ingenuously optimistic view of the world: the land resists human efforts to live off it; women bear children in pain; nature and our own bodies impose all sorts of limitations; there is the universal destiny of death (Gen. 3:16–19). But the fact that nature is inhospitable and dangerous does not mean that the world is ruled by "evil" powers, nor that it has come like that from God; rather these characteristics of nature are the result of sin (see Rom. 5:12–21; Wisd. of Sol. 1:13–15; 2:22–4); they have come about because human beings—individually and collectively—have abused and continue to abuse their freedom before the creator and their dominion over creation; they have come about because creation "was made the victim of frustration . . . because of him who made it so; yet always there was hope, because the universe itself is to be freed from the shackles of mortality and enter upon the liberty and splendour of the children of God" (Rom. 8:20–21). And so when the prophets of Israel, preaching conversion and hope, glimpsed the Kingdom to come, they saw the people set free, men and women with new hearts, and the whole of creation restored, welcoming and fruitful (see Isa. 11:6–8; 35). And when Jesus the Christ appeared proclaiming the imminent Reign of God, he confirmed his proclamation with deeds and "signs" that were not only of "forgiveness of sins" and reconciliation with God, but also, and by the same token, of the integral restoration of human beings—in mind, body and society—and of the reconciliation of humankind with the natural world. Jesus embarked on his mission and devoted himself to it "even to death on a cross," not only "for forgiveness of sins" but also to "take away the sin of the world," to open the way to this new "freedom of the children of God" which will be shared by the whole of creation, at the service of humankind (see Matt. 26:28; John 1:29; Rom. 8:19–23). And this same Jesus Christ, as risen Lord, is in his person and together with all of us, the true and final Adam, for and through whom all things were made, and to whom "God has subjected everything under his feet," even "the last enemy to be destroyed ... death" (Col. 1:16; 1 Cor. 15:27; see Ps. 8:6–7).

2. GOD AND SOCIETY

The second section of this chapter on "God and the world" deals with the world as humankind's surroundings, the collective dimension of humankind itself, the "world" as human society. Applying the same scheme as in the previous section will show popular understanding of both dimensions of the world—as nature and as society—to be interwoven and superimposed on each other.

(a) Cultural Process

The first section outlined the changes that have taken place in the life, work and mentality of the people over two generations, between the peasant grandparents and the urban youth of today, seeing how this affected their view of the natural world. The same process of change affects their view of the human world, their relations with their fellow men and women, with the order and institutions of society.

The "old-style" families still exist, where the peasant structure has been least affected by the wave of new urban culture, where changes in the pattern of work and social organization have been more gradual or have impinged less on the consciousness, world view and daily lives of peasant families. There are still patriarchal families, with roles distributed in clear and unalterable hierarchical patterns: the indisputable authority of the "head of the household," his work as the only source of income, the licence allowed to him as a result; the submission of the wife, who does all the housework, is exclusively responsible for the upbringing of the children; the total dependence of the children, lasting well beyond adolescence, particularly grown-up daughters. . . . Peasant families are still dependent on the "bosses," not only for work and income, but in many other important dimensions of social and cultural life. There is an unbridgeable, "eternal" gap perceived by the mass of the poor between themselves and groups privileged by wealth, education and power; this is a traditional popular understanding of the order, laws and institutions of society as a whole as coming from above, being understood and manipulated by those at the top, while those at the bottom can only submit.

There is still a massive persistence of this submissive mentality in the "townships" or barrios. This mentality has been gradually ousted by new experiences and new collective practices, but it has also been restored by fear and the traumas of bloody repression by so many regimes, and it has been reinforced by the pressure of the dominant ideology, which uses every means to hammer home the message that any rebellion, resistance or dissidence against the established order is criminal or deeply perverse.

Nevertheless, those peasants who have emigrated to the cities have discovered a tradition of working-class struggle there, along with trade unions, and a more critical attitude to employers and the dominant system of production, and this has given them a sharper sense of being part of an exploited and repressed social class. To a certain extent, this has happened in the countryside too, through new forms of social and work organization: unionization, agrarian reform, cooperatives and the like. Such experiences leave their mark, even if they are subsequently overturned. In the cities, too, there are a host of neighbourhood projects, which have sprung up from the need simply to survive, to fight for one's rights, to defend one's cultural inheritance. Young people in Latin America have grown to consciousness of their situation through having access to secondary education and then through informal and alternative channels; they have learned something of the social and political history of their countries, and have developed critical techniques for judging the present structure of the societies they live in. On top of all this, there are the more directly political popular organizations and movements, in which significant minorities from all generations have taken part, thereby experiencing indignation in the face of social injustice, utopic longings for an egalitarian society, organizational ability, and the fact of engaged struggle to change existing society.

Such experiences involve a whole change of attitude: a new way of relating to one's neighbours, of being a person in one's social milieu, of viewing one's responsibilities and possibilities in relation to other people. Before (and this is still true of some in the older generations), just as people felt themselves part of nature as a given whole, seen as something with its necessary order and unchanging behaviour, so they felt part of society, also seen as an organic whole, stratified and hierarchical, which had "always been like that" and had its "natural" order and way of functioning. Now, on the other hand, and especially among the young, people are standing back in their appreciation of the ruling social order, learning to put it into focus, to compare it with different experiences and to imagine alternative futures. We now know that society as it is has not always been like that, that it is the product of an evolutionary process, and of applications of force that need not have happened that way and that tomorrow can perhaps be reversed. We no longer see society as a "natural" order established forever, but as the product of a history, in which the fears and interests, powers and alliances of different groups play their part. Present-day society is not an "established order," but a stage in a process, with an organizational structure that is questionable and replaceable, something whose continuance in its present unjust form in fact constitutes a challenge to our common responsibility as human beings. In our present understanding, individuals are emerging far more clearly as subjects, and existing society as a historical reality: the product of a past history, transient, open to change by us in the direction of a different future.

This is where we see the importance of the social sciences

and of politics, as instruments for gaining greater knowledge of the mechanics of society and for being able to exert influence over its development. And this is why groups privileged by the existing order—particularly when they exercise power without opposition—are concerned to discredit the social sciences and condemn politics. It is also why those sectors of the oppressed people with most historical knowledge are tempted to attribute almost absolute value to them. What remains a fact—and one from which there is no going back—is that we have discovered that society is a human product and a human task; we now understand that we all, and especially those majorities who are now held down, share the responsibility for making the society of tomorrow more human: its economy organized for solidarity rather than exploitation, power in it exercised more by participation than by domination.

Previously, our image of society and of the individual's place in it was almost exclusively vertical, made up of relationships of authority and obedience. It was seen as natural to belong to a nation as subjects of a monarch, to belong to a business enterprise as employees of a boss, to belong to a parish or religious community as a parish priest's "flock" or under obedience to a religious superior. Now, we are developing a new understanding of the basic equality and universal solidarity of all human beings. Our view of a truly human society and the place of each one of us in it takes horizontal relationships as basic, and it emphasizes ties of neighbourliness and reciprocity and common and shared responsibilities. We understand our belonging to a nation, organization or community as stemming from citizenship, partnership or brotherhood and sisterhood, all of which bring equal rights and obligations; we value the horizontal ties of solidarity and communion above all. This is not to deny that some individuals or groups have special gifts and tasks, that some must exercise authority in society. But we see such authority as legitimate only when mandated by the people, when such individuals are elected or recognized by the consensus of the community. In the family too—where there are natural ties of authority and dependence—the traditional machismo is gradually giving way to more equal and reciprocal relationships between the partners, to communication with the children, enabling them to grow in freedom and emerge as genuine friends of their parents.

(b) Crisis of "God"

In this cultural process, the traditional experience of God also has to change or lose relevance. The received manner of seeing God's authority, will and power over the social order and the relationships of everyday life either has to change profoundly, or come to be seen as a tiresome obstacle standing in the way of more human relationships.

Many older people still experience human dependence on the traditional order and authorities of their social world as something imbued with deep sacral and religious import. The often yawning differences of standards of living and possibilities between rich and poor, the division of work and social roles into master and slave, the monopoly held on decision-making and the accumulation of power in the hands of a privileged few, the alternation between oppression and relaxation in the "national economy"—all are seen as part of a sacred order and the will of God, as the only wise order for the body social and the most suitable for all its members, even those apparently least favoured by the status quo. From this it follows that everyone's duty—in humility before God and in obedience to God's will—is to conform to one's inherited state, act in accordance with one's "civil duty" and accept the wages or handouts offered by the established order.

The experience of belonging to a human society patterned on the model of the patriarchal family places emphasis on vertical relationships and dependence. God sits on the summit, above the authorities, guaranteeing the established order and directing the body social through its appointed powers. Those in command—father, parish priest, boss, governor—are seen as "vicarious" authorities, God's representatives, "sacraments" (signs and instruments) of the higher government exercised over human society by the almighty. So God is cast in the image and likeness of the powers and authorities of this world: the super-governor, top boss, universal father.

So, when we distance ourselves critically from the order and hierarchies of present society, see the differences and powers in existing society as a product of history, take stock of institution- alized violence and injustice, conceive the utopia of a society of equality and solidarity, discover our own possibilities of organ- ization to withstand and change the existing order of things — then there is clearly not only a crisis of our submission to the ruling order and the authorities that keep it in place, but also of submission to God, or at least to our image of a God who legitimizes that order and requires us to submit to it. So our relationship with society, our social practices and our very way of living with our neighbours produce a crisis of our faith in God the Father, almighty king. More precisely, it produces a crisis of the image of God as a father who protects and provides for our needs, but at the same time keeps us in submission and does not let us grow up. It produces a crisis in the image of God as a governor who safeguards the order and security of the social body, but does so as a universal ruler who imposes his own will as law, and who acts like a supreme "intelligence service" to seek out and repress all forms of rebellion.

Such an image of the almighty does not account for the whole of the traditional experience of God held by the people. It is, though, a major component, found in the humble people who rely on a certain line of official church preaching, and still more in the "Catholic" ideology of the ruling classes. But the people also have a countervailing image of a "God of the poor," before whom all are equal, who goes with and gives courage to the dispossessed and downtrodden, and joy to those who share. And this God produces the conviction that the greed of the rich, their exploitation of the poor, and the pomp of the powerful are things of the devil.[3]

The superseding of this traditional image of God the Father should not be thought to have removed all positive valuation of the idea of fatherhood and authority in our new suburban cul- ture, especially among the young. On the contrary, their very frustrations — in the daily family round and the broader histor- ical perspective — often feed a nostalgia for a father who will help them to grow and be free, who will be a friend; a nostalgia for leaders and governors who will be truly at the service of the people and have real authority, not just power and force.

The following, then, are the seeds and supports for rediscovering the good news of Jesus Christ: God the merciful Father, the Reign of God and God's justice, God as one who wills a free people sharing the fullness of life among all its members.

(c) New Perspectives

The crisis of "God" that affects our relations with society offers the greatest opportunity for purifying our Christian faith and opening ourselves to a new experience of the living and true God. It is the greatest opportunity because by guiding us to rediscover and examine the biblical tradition of the God who sets the people free and of the Reign of God "on earth as in heaven," it is pointing us in the direction of themes that are central to the Bible as a dynamic whole. Reading the Bible in the base communities among the poor, three aspects stand out:

1. We truly come to know the God of the Bible — experience God as a living reality, become involved in communion with God — when we fully realize that this God has chosen to intervene in our collective history, has "judged" it, in order to free groups of people within it who are oppressed, exploited and scattered, in order to make them a people of free beings in solidarity. This state of oppression and servitude has been "sacralized" by alienated worship of false gods, those of the power and private wealth of the rulers: Pharaoh and the magnates of Egypt, the corrupt kings and power-seeking groups in Israel itself, the heads and ruling classes of the great empires. Our new state of organization and freedom, sharing and solidarity, is linked to the encounter and covenant offered us by the true God, the God of humble service and goods shared among the poor of the earth. Liberation and access to the Kingdom of God involve abandoning the idols of domination and massacre, and being converted to the service of the living and true God, the God of solidarity and fully human life for all. Reading the Bible today in the context of our believing progress as a people, we do not confuse our Christian faith with our task of collective liberation; nor do we reduce it to this task. Neither, though, can we separate the spiritual and religious dimension from the temporal and social, experience of and faithfulness to the living God

from commitment to the liberation of the oppressed and the struggle for a just and equal society.

2. So the active presence and call of the only true God are found not in the "great ones" of the earth, not in the "sacred power" of human hierarchies, not in the elitist culture and prestige of the "upper classes"; it is found in the neighbour in need, recognized and served as such, and in the crowd of the poor and marginalized, with their privations and their hopes. It is not found in the mendacious order and sneering security of a repressive, class-divided society, but in the longing and struggle for a more just and human way of living together, by means of love and self-sacrifice; not in the ethos of competition and privatization, not in technological progress for the sake of the refined well-being of a privileged minority, but in the people's experience of solidarity and community, where all feel responsible for one another and learn to share goods and services, in the mobilizing utopia of universal equality.

Reading the Bible and discovering its living tradition from the standpoint of the poor show that, if there is a "sacral" dimension and a "religious" experience attached to the power of rulers, to repressive society and individualistic acquisition of wealth, it is the experience of a negative and perverse sacredness: the idolatry of riches, the gods of oppression, the "Prince of this world." These are mendacious and death-dealing gods. The true God, the God of life, is the God of the Beatitudes, of the Kingdom preached to the poor and those who hunger and thirst after justice, the God who raised him who was crucified by the powers and sacred hierarchies of this world, the "God all in all" of universal reconciliation and peace.

3. From among the repressed and impoverished of the world, this true God gives the strength and wisdom of the Spirit, shares out gifts and talents, summoning human responsibility to reverse the social dynamic of envy and domination, to build a structure of justice and sharing in love. This responsibility — of individuals, groups, whole peoples — involves generous and intelligent human response to God's summons, to the divine initiative of the first liberation and the founding covenant, and to the decisive liberation and new covenant in Jesus Christ. Such a response involves being converted from idols to serve the living

and true God, reversing repeated apostasies in order to perse-
vere in faithfulness to the God of the covenant. Or, put the
other way round, it involves conversion and faithfulness to the
living God, which are verified in solidarity shown through love
for the needy and a commitment to justice in favour of the
oppressed.

These three aspects are inseparable, and documented
throughout the entire Bible, from the foundational event of the
exodus from Egypt and the covenant on Sinai, to the certain
hope of the new heavens and new earth where justice will dwell
and God will be "all in all," via the good news of the Kingdom
and the paschal event of Jesus Christ. This is the line followed
by the historical traditions of Israel and the laws governing how
the Israelites were to live together in the promised land; this is
the content of the preaching of the prophets, the prayers of the
Psalms, the hope of Revelation; it is, finally, the good news
brought by Jesus, preached by the apostles and practised by the
early Christian communities. The true God, then, is always —
and ever more clearly and more radically — the God who liberates the oppressed, whom we see and are challenged by in the
poor of the earth, who wants the genuine religious worship
shown in mercy for those in need and a commitment to justice
and peace in our world.[4] But there is more to be said about the
theological root of Christian life in community and the universal
human calling to live in community.

4. The content of all biblical revelation reaches its fullness
and is summed up in the "good news" that Jesus proclaimed to
the poor and outcasts of his people, in the "message" that the
witnesses to the risen Christ began to spread through the under-
world of the Roman Empire: that God is coming to reign, that
this Reign has already begun in the humble practice of Jesus, a
radical subversion of the hierarchies and powers of this world;
that the Father has raised his servant Jesus, whom the tribunals
of his nation sentenced, revindicating him as his Son and Messiah for all peoples; that the God and Father of Jesus, the Messiah, has become our Father and that we are all brothers and
sisters; that the Spirit, through outer signs and actions within
us, is the witness and invisible agent of this deep transformation
of life and human society, in which we are all children and all

free, heirs and co-workers together of and for the fullness of the Kingdom of justice. (Of course, this transformation is embryonic and in the realm of hope: it does not suppress the kingdoms of this world or remove the tremendous weight of injustice and domination; it does not exempt us from intelligent effort, or from sacrifice. But it is a change that goes to the root of how human beings live together—spiritually, bodily, socially, historically—and is destined to transform the entire tree, from the sap to the branches.)

At the heart of the gospel is the identity of the God of the Kingdom with the Father of Jesus Christ, his "Abba" (the Aramaic word the children of Palestine used as a familiar way of addressing their fathers, and which the gospel tradition shows Jesus using to address God). "Kingdom" is a term belonging to the political order; "Abba" evokes the intimacy of the family. And in effect, the sort of "kingship" Jesus shows in his practice as Messiah of the poor, and the experience of "sonship" he reveals to "the least of the brethren," do not bring the world a new "hierarchy" (the "sacred power" which has been so important for the self-understanding and internal workings of the Catholic Church since the Middle Ages—"hierarchy" being a word derived not from the New Testament, but from Platonism and Eastern mysticism, particularly the Gnostic currents, which underpinned the "monarchianism" [central power of an individual] of the Roman Empire),[5] a new religious dependence that leaves human beings and the humble people as minors. Quite the reverse: they produce a deep dynamism of equality, of service and communion among equals. The servant Jesus, the Messiah as persecuted prophet who ushers in the Reign of God in this way, is God's "beloved Son," who is now seated at the right hand of the Father. Jesus did not call his disciples and emissaries slaves but friends, his brothers and sisters. The fact that we all have a single Father and a single teacher does not authorize some to set themselves up as fathers and teachers of the rest: on the contrary, it is an impulse to companionship, to deep friendship, to humble service among equals.

This is because, in the final analysis, the root content of Jesus' message—and of the mystery of God—is love. And love that is truly worthy of the name, the love of which God consists and that has been revealed to us in Jesus Christ, is not ultimately a tumbling cascade of "benefits," monarchy and subordination, but a communion among equals: Father, Son and Spirit; the Spirit in us and we in the Son face to face with the Father.[6]

5. Naturally—and as part of the mystery of love and life— this communion among equals does not suppress the original difference between persons; it does not suppress the gratuitousness of the gift that brings communion into being. The Father goes on being the Father, Father also and above all of the Son; the Lord and master goes on being Lord and master, especially of his companions and friends, among whom he acts as one who serves. God goes on being God, also and above all of the creatures God has chosen and sanctified and loves "in the Son." But, difference itself has been taken up and transformed in this dynamism of communion among equals, producing inexhaustible wonder and greater joy in love.

On the modest level of our own lives, this is what we can experience through being called to teach others, provided we do it with real devotion; more generally, it is what young people can experience when they themselves become parents. In both cases, our concern is not to affirm our own authority, to maintain distance or possession. On the contrary, this is an urge to give the best of oneself, so as to enable children or pupils to grow, to open out to others who have more to give, to be free. It is the impatient longing and hope for our "little ones" to become our equals and better than we as soon as possible, and—if they freely wish to—become our friends and companions.

Family life for our young people today is often so traumatic that becoming parents themselves seems to be a better way of coming to understand what it means to say that God is "our Father." It is possible for young people to see the image of God as Father in their earthly fathers, but—and especially in a situation where so many have been deprived of their earthly fathers—their own experience of parenthood is often the better way. This would seem to be the main way suggested in the gospel: "Would any of you give a stone to your son when he asks for bread? . . . As bad as you are, you know how to give good things to your children. How much more, then, will your Father in heaven give good things to those who ask him!" (Matt. 7:9–

11). In the Sermon on the Mount itself, we are taught to ask the Father for "our daily bread," to "forgive us our debts as we forgive those [our children?] who are in debt to us" (6:11–12). We are summoned, then, to be like the father in the parable of the prodigal son, who tenderly welcomes and forgives, who will not even think of leaving his child in the condition of a slave, but forgets and orders a feast . . . and expects the other son — "you are always with me and all I have is yours" — to do as much for his returning brother (Luke 15:11–32).

CHAPTER IV

God and Human Beings

We saw in the last chapter that the God of nature—understood in a Christian sense—concerns and challenges us radically, as our creator and Lord of human history. And—seen in the light of the Bible—the God of our collective history, who calls us together as a people and leads us to the Kingdom of the promise, both sets us free and sets us on the journey toward our fullness as a community of persons. "God and the world" dealt with our human, real world: the world we discover in the light of faith as both gift and task given to us by God on our journey toward fullness of life and living together.

This chapter on "God and human beings" starts more directly from human life itself, from ourselves and from each one of us as we see ourselves, with our daily occupations and concerns. I hope thereby—without separating this dimension from the one studied in the last chapter—to reach further into human "hearts," to examine how our cultural processes affect our experience of God on this level. This will, I hope, help to open up new ways of glimpsing, slightly more directly, the "heart" of the God and Father of Jesus Christ, the God of all and of each one of us.

1. GOD AND HUMAN ACTIVITY

Let us look first at ourselves as working beings, acting in more or less methodical and constant ways on nature and in relation to our fellow beings; at ourselves working to sustain our own lives and those of our group; at ourselves devoting our efforts to making our own lives, as individuals and in community, more human within the context of the society in which we live.

(a) Cultural Process

There are two aspects or dimensions to be tackled here: the first, relating to work and the daily struggle for subsistence; the second, relating to the authority of a doctrine or the witness of a practice.

1. Activity, human "doing," is not something external to our "being" and self-realization. Of course, work or action does not account for the whole of human life. But we live and commune in and through our activity, which is not merely making or achieving things, but "making" and achieving ourselves, effectively "building" the human community and planning for our collective future. This is a social and anthropological truth that has been clearly recognized in the official teaching of the church. It is, however, a truth that has only recently been appreciated by us, churchmen and churchwomen, as something applicable to our own lives and to what we teach. Till recently, in ecclesiastical circles more absorbed in doctrine, this truth was seen as tinged with Promethean pride or Pelagianism,[1] and those who held it were suspected of having been infiltrated by humanistic and atheistic materialism.

What we are looking at is not so much a cultural process undergone by "the people" as a change experienced by the "consecrated people" of the church as they draw closer to the people, learning their values and the actual conditions of their lives. We, the church agents who make this approach, tend, from our basically middle-class background and the place our ministry gives us in society, to value intellectual and verbal activity and to look down on manual labour. As people devoted to "things of the spirit," free of family responsibilities and usually of the need to earn our own living, we can easily hover above the "material problems" of our people. With our backgrounds, and the sort of seminary or convent education we received, we found it difficult to interest ourselves in the sort of work done by "outsiders" and its material results. Our concern was focussed (still is, in many cases) both nearer than work, on the field of personal motivation and intention, and beyond it, on the ordering of all good actions and sufferings in this life to a higher destiny, that of transcendent salvation. Catholic catechisms and the official wording of the Roman liturgy still point in this direction. The daily lives of ordinary people, with their concerns and duties, the world of work for those who have work and the tremendous vacuum in the lives of those who have none — all this is regarded as something "outside," relegated to a "servile" or "profane" level.

Gradually, however, the poor themselves, through their dramatic presence and wisdom, have come to teach us the importance in human terms of their daily struggle for subsistence; they have shown us the sacred dignity of work, even alienated and exploited as it is — when it is there — in our free-market civilization. Work itself, however humiliated, dignifies and builds up human beings, at the same time as it wears them out. Our true concern has to be with the results and concrete utility of human work and activity, as these respond to the vital needs of individuals and groups. These needs may be viewed as immediate, lowly or "material," but people live out and work out their lives in the hard daily struggle to satisfy them, even on the most basic level.

2. Work and, more generally, all human activity or actions suppose a goal and more or less conscious decisions, within the limitations of the possibilities offered. I am not referring just to the various methods or techniques applicable to a particular branch of work, but to a more basic level, that of the deep desires, understanding and decision-making we bring to our activity: what to do and what to leave undone, what activity we devote our main energies to, what we hope to achieve from it, how we approach our work and with whom. So we need to ask: What weighs most with us or influences us most in choosing one course or another? What models or criteria guide our actions? What factors matter to us, or whom do we listen to, supposing we are not deciding alone or purely on grounds of immediate gain?

This aspect certainly shows major changes in the cultural

development of the people themselves. Previously, as still with older people, it was simply a matter of doing "what had to be done," and of doing it "as it had always been done." Peasants ploughed the land the way they had learned from their elders; they knew this way and would find it hard to learn another. Young people learned, at home and in school, how to behave, what things they could do and how to do them. Actions, behaviour in the family or neighbourhood group, moral conduct, manual labour or any activity had to be done according to certain guidelines; they had to conform to received patterns or norms, those laid down by the authorities. Society itself, leaving aside a certain philosophical and ideological pluralism that rarely affected the majority, handed down a fairly coherent scale of values and more or less coherent rules of behaviour. So the key words in education and apprenticeship were "tradition," "authority," "docility" and "reproduction."

Now, on the other hand, young people grow up in less close-knit families, with serious problems of communication with their elders. The view of the world and the discipline formal education tries to impose on them do not jell with the values they experience at home, nor precisely with those that invade the home through television. So young people look to their peer groups for a way of living together and a meaning to life that they cannot find from the muddled and contradictory adult world.

In these conditions, there do not appear to be any readymade, "sure" doctrines or criteria to guide young people in their behaviour and activities. The various "authorities" proposed to them have to compete with contradictory proposals, and all too often fall victim to their own incoherence. In the best cases, the criteria put forward by adults can be seen to be genuine, on account of the genuineness of the lives and commitment of those who propose them. But this does not necessarily mean that they will appear valid in the same form for young people, who know they live in very different circumstances. Just because something was sure and good in other times, in the circumstances and understanding of people then, does not necessarily mean that it will be so for "us" today, in the conditions in which "we" have to live.

So what is left is a quest: searching for what will best respond to young people's longings for life and commitment; trying and testing the truth of the various propositions on offer; experiencing as an individual and in groups what will in practice prove truthful and fruitful, for oneself and for the sake of the future of all the oppressed people. So we can offer a new series of key words, in counterpoint to those enumerated above: for "tradition," read "experience"; for "authority," "witness"; for "docility," "criticism"; for "reproduction," "creativity."

(b) Crisis of "God"

Here we need to look in turn at the two aspects of the crisis, deriving each from one of the processes described above: first, from the distance between "our" ("spiritual persons") God and the daily concerns of our people; second, from the contrast between our young people's quest and a God handed down by tradition and authority.

1. If our "spiritual lives," our own experience of God and religious language, fail to give due weight to the material lives and concerns of the people, to the precariousness of their lives and their struggle for subsistence, then we shall fail to engage the real lives and concerns of the people we are supposed to minister to. We shall find that "things of the spirit," and even God, seem not to interest people. The ways we experience and speak about God may seem beautiful, proper to our condition of "consecrated persons." Deep down, however, they will be disqualified as "too highfalutin for us," too abstract and distant, with no "hold" in the situation of oppression the people know, no pertinence to their real needs—often life or death matters. We shall then find ourselves in the position of people trying to sell something for which there is no demand.

Then we, as religious and missionaries, will be in crisis, apparently cornered between two alternatives: either we cling to "our God" and fall back on received forms of spiritual life and preaching, throwing in our lot with a few chosen souls and, under the guise of facing up to the materialism of the masses, abandoning "these cursed people who have no knowledge of the Law" (John 7:49) to the fate they deserve; or we begin to doubt

the relevance of this "our God" to this oppressed people, and
so leave "our God" on one side, the better to devote ourselves
to the task of advancing and liberating the people. In fact, however, the crisis in both alternatives is that of our own limited
experience and inadequate expression of God: as the most high,
as the God of my soul and of eternal life, as ultimate meaning
and universal judge of my life and the world, beyond life and
the world. So we need to ask ourselves how far this image of
God really comes from the biblical tradition, and how far it is
consistent today with the faith of the simple people (see Matt.
11:25–7); or to what extent it rather reflects a philosophical
doctrine and a mystical tradition marked by Platonist dualism –
the religious ideology of a "class" cut off from the needs and
sufferings of the poor mass of the people.

2. As to the second aspect, it is not hard to understand how
the crisis of tradition and authority – a crisis that marks the cultural development of the people – affects the viability of a God
received precisely through tradition and authority. In such an
open and mobile society, where so few values and norms are
recognized as universal and permanent, and young people are
besieged with such disparate and contradictory messages, it is
understandable that a God taught by parents and schoolmasters,
preached by priests, will not readily be accepted; it is understandable that it no longer makes sense to believe in God "like
everyone else does and always has done."

So here, especially among young people, there is a crisis of
"God" as a dogma taught and a universal law for the world.
And here we need to ask how much more "knowledge" of the
living God, in the Bible and in those with real experience of
God, is than mere acceptance of common religious belief; how
much more Christian faith is than merely "believing all that Holy
Mother Church teaches and orders us to believe"; how much
more the "way" and practice of Christians are than merely
"putting into practice" commandments handed down and rules
laid down by religious authority.

(c) New Perspectives

These two aspects of the crisis of "God" converge in the
cultural situation of young people faced with the proclamation

of the God of Jesus Christ. They account for their difficulty when faced with a proclamation that generally appears so "spiritual," so theoretical and ethereal in relation to their real interests and conditions of life, all wrapped up in their general reluctance to accept any teaching handed down by their elders or any "authority." But it is just here that new perspectives open up for proclaiming a more evangelical and liberating God.

Faced with these two aspects of the crisis, we need to pick out here two aspects of the biblical experience of God that have become especially pertinent to us today: first, the experience of a God of concrete human life, rather than of the "spiritual life" or "heaven"; and second, the experience of a God of actual people and particular communities, rather than of general theories or received doctrines.

1. The biblical term "God of life" is not a metaphysical definition dreamt up by a spiritual elite. It is a popular designation, expressing the experience of a people closely tied to the soil, to the basic needs and joys of bodily and community life, an experience of God woven into the "material" weft of everyday life: food or hunger, health or sickness, friendship or quarrels, work and the struggle for subsistence, shared poverty or festivity. This is a basic aspect of our rediscovery of the "humanity" of the God of the Bible. This is a God who not only created us "in the image and likeness of God," but is concerned with the details of our daily lives — family, dealings with neighbours, work, living — and looks to us to be faithful to the covenant in these areas. This God rejoices in our growth and our happiness, in how we feel in our bodies and our communities; who "blesses" us with the beasts and the land to care for, to work, and to enjoy their fruits giving thanks and sharing our pleasures with family and friends. And equally this God commits the faithful to serve their neighbours who suffer poverty, loneliness, oppression, in the material and social senses of these words.

This experience of a "human" God, founded on Israel's oldest religious tradition and deepened by prophets and teachers of wisdom throughout its history, reaches its clearest and most radical experience in Jesus of Nazareth. Judaic society and culture of his time showed a very clear distinction between worship and secular life, between priesthood and laity, between the religious elites and the "cursed people with no knowledge of the Law." In this social and religious context, Jesus was born and lived as a lay person; he immersed himself in the lives and concerns of the ordinary people, revealing directly to them — and not through "religious" words or symbols — the love of the Father and what they had to do to inherit his coming Kingdom; he performed "signs" that were not ritual gestures, but human ones, to heal and save men and women suffering from being destitute, outcasts, oppressed by devils; he relativized all religious practices or "observances" in terms of their usefulness to the health or dignity of actual people; he taught his disciples to recognize his risen presence and the Father's love, not in the Temple and its rites or in solitary contemplation, but in those who suffer or share, in the living community of his followers.[2]

Work and the "material" dimension of life belong to corporeal and social life; they are some of the goods that go to make up life itself and life in community, goods that are a part, an element, of life itself. Those of us who are not poor — particularly if we are professional church people — typically regard lack of work, exploited work, hunger and malnutrition, lack of shoes or shelter in winter, lack of a roof over one's head . . . as purely "material" problems. The poor know this is not true. They know that they are problems which affect the whole of life, human problems. The fact is that everything which serves or affects subsistence and the basics of life is also spiritual. If anything stands out from an unbiased reading of the Gospels, it is this: that Jesus knew this better than anyone; that this is obvious to the merciful gaze of that God and Father of whom he spoke, whom he knew better than anyone.

So, in the conditions of poverty prevailing today, the whole biblical tradition, and the good news brought by Jesus above all, invite us to seek out God, to be faithful and bear witness to God's liberating presence in the very "material" substance of life as lived by the people: in their struggle to provide food for their families, to put a roof over their heads; in paid work or the endless quest for any honest way of providing the basics of life. They urge us to seek out the God who is our Father/Mother too, to bear witness, with respect, understanding and commitment, to those most in need, to those most impoverished, starting with their most basic bodily and social needs. They challenge us to "make the experiment" of the God of life, to show forth this God in a generous, clearheaded and sharing endeavour to humanize this world of ours, to the benefit above all of the oppressed and marginalized masses. They challenge us to undertake a concerted struggle against all that destroys their lives and militates against all human community: unemployment and the extreme poverty it brings, rooted in an economic system — national and international — of exploitation; repression, with its extremes of torture and political assassination, terror and mass paralysis, rooted in a despotic and excluding sociopolitical system.

It is in this matter of everyday life, in service to the bodies of the needy, in the struggle for a more just and equitable society, that we meet and contemplate the God of life. And this meeting will in turn give new depth to our daily lives, bring a new joy in our service, new hope to our struggle.

2. The Bible, we have seen, does not refer to God as the key to any general theory, or as the nucleus of any doctrine that has to be learned and handed on. The Bible deals with the history of a people, with the actions of particular individuals and communities, with the God of these individuals and communities, seen acting and challenging us through them.

Those who recognize this God are witnesses. All believers can in effect witness to the fact that God, before being "my" God, was for me the God of someone, or of a specific community, the God of people who not only spoke to me of God, but who showed God in their way of living, of trusting, of giving themselves to others. Some of these people will certainly also have taught me doctrine about God, and ways of approaching God in prayer. Although both these things are important, the likelihood is that much of this language about God and pious practice corresponded to another sensibility and another time, and has gradually been left behind. The basic fact remains, however: that these people, through the faith that gave meaning to their whole lives of love and service, were for me the men and women "of God," those who brought me to the meeting with the "our" God who has become "my" God.

This is how God was "known" in the Bible, through being

"the God of Abraham, Isaac and Jacob," the God of Moses, of Samuel, of Elijah. . . . This does not mean that everything in the behaviour and piety of Abraham, Moses or Elijah is put forward for us to imitate; nor is everything in their stories edifying. But they were "the friends of God," those "who walked with God," who could entrust themselves to and put themselves completely in God's hands, who believed in their God's promise to the chosen people "against all hope," against the prevailing climate and to the end.

When the Letter to the Hebrews sets out a reflection on the basic elements of our faith, this is precisely what it recounts (see Heb. 11:1 – 12:3). It brings out the memory of the long line of men and women who, throughout the course of the history of their people, "by faith" won kingdoms, brought justice, brought the promises to fulfillment . . . and were mocked, whipped, imprisoned, exiled, cut to pieces. . . . It speaks of the "cloud of innumerable witnesses" who sustain our faith. It refers us above all to Jesus, "the founder of our faith . . . who will bring it to completion." "His" God—the God he invoked and who gave meaning to his whole life, the God he showed forth in all that he did, even to giving himself up to death on the cross—is the God who has come to be "our" God and Father. And today, in the footsteps of Jesus, we too can see a "cloud of witnesses" in our suffering people, men and women who speak to us in so many ways, through their manner of life and of giving up their lives, of the living and liberating God—and speak better than many wise and authorized experts.

The testimony provided by these witnesses is above all that of their actions, their way of life; these are presented to us as a possible way, a working hypothesis, for us to travel and test. If you don't know that it can make sense to risk your life for love and justice; if you don't know if anyone is listening to your prayers, then test these things in your own life. This is the way of Jesus Christ: the New Testament does not speak, as we do, of "Christianity" in its abstract and authoritarian sense of a "doctrine of Christ," but of the good news of the Kingdom, of the "witness" of the resurrection, or simply of the "way." The "way" here means the alternative to which we can commit our lives for the sake of the hope of justice for the poor and life for

the world. We, each one of us, have to put it to the test, through
our actions and commitment. It is up to us to show the life of
the risen Christ in us through giving life and hope to others; to
find out if, in daily commitment in the midst of contradictions,
we can discover the beatitude, the joy of God.[3]

2. GOD AND PERSONAL FREEDOM

The God of nature and society, as perceived from the biblical
tradition, is a God who sets us to work to earn our living through
using our intelligence, who urges us to serve others by attending
first to their most basic needs and rights, who commits us to
work in solidarity to move the present world in the direction of
the Kingdom. All this means a call to the conscience and responsibility we all possess as human beings; we have to make deliberate decisions, vital choices which involve a selfless
commitment of our lives themselves. This in turn gives us a
better idea of the being and nature of this God who challenges
us in this way, awakening our conscience and provoking us to
respond from the depth of our human nature: our personal freedom.

(a) Cultural Process

In the traditional culture of the poor, the objective conditions
of oppression and dependency weigh so heavily that work is a
necessity or slavery, life itself is experienced as at best something
passively undergone, or at worst an actual passion, a *via crucis*.
Individual human lives and the history of the collectivity are
seen, like the natural cycles, as fulfilling a destiny, something
preordained because "it had to be so," "it was written," "God
willed it." . . . People's virtue, or correct attitude as Christians,
could emerge only in humble resignation to this servitude, in
calm acceptance of one's own destiny, in trusting self-abandon-
ment to the will of God, who had everything worked out for the
good of the chosen. Many spiritualities — those of old religious
congregations and those of some new lay "renewal" movements — speak of "the will of God" or "God's plan" in this way:
as a plan that we simply have to carry out since it has all been

decided in advance, as though the entire script had been written and we were merely being invited to act out our parts faithfully.

In the new urban popular culture, especially in the more thinking sectors of young people, there is a growing tendency to face up to life as a challenge to human responsibility, a responsibility now seen as having connotations of critique, initiative and creativity. This amounts to having a purpose in life which motivates us, guides us in finding a way of living, sharing and carrying out a particular line of service. This purpose in life is not something that has been drawn up in advance, laid down by society, those in authority or a "transcendent will"; it is rather something that each individual or couple has to discover and plan out for themselves, a path that is kept open by treading it. Of course there are factors we have to take into account, being realistic: our strengths and weaknesses, the opportunities on offer, the needs of the people, and the like. But, taking these factors into account, we have to see ourselves, know ourselves, judge ourselves with kindness.

On the collective level too, we can speak of a "historical purpose." This is not something as specific or contingent as a political aim or party programme. It is both broader and longer-term in scope: it means something like the people themselves reflecting on their state of oppression, or on the strength they have if they act together, and projecting their ideas of equality and justice into the future, sketching out the image of a different society while at the same time bringing it partially into being through their daily lives and struggles. Though such an image is not something that can be found actually defined and operating, there is such a "purpose" taking general shape among and mobilizing the peoples of Latin America. It is a sign of the people maturing, ceasing to be a disparate, passive and malleable mass, becoming a network of communications and organizations, becoming more conscious and articulate, taking their destiny into their own hands.

These two levels, the personal and the collective, do not have separate purposes, and one purpose cannot in fact be understood without the other. There can be no personal growth and self-understanding in terms of working out a truly fruitful purpose in life if they are not conceived and carried out in solidarity

with and within the framework of the "historical purpose" of
the oppressed people. And the collective purpose, for its part,
cannot be clarified and take shape in practice without more and
more individuals and groups working out a lucid purpose in life
for themselves.

If there is a tendency in this direction among many individuals
and among the people as such, this is not a general and automatic development; nor is it even something that can be found
among the majority. The "cultural process" I am referring to is
the opening out that is found, in principle, in urban popular
culture and especially among young people; this is an opening
out to the possibilities for steering one's life in one direction or
another and to the need, even, for making a choice, on whatever
level of consciousness or depth, that will give meaning to one's
life. These possibilities are evidently largely frustrated by the
objective conditions in which most young people in our cities
are forced to live. But in spite of that, these possibilities continue
to grow in the understanding of young people, who see the challenge posed to their personal growth and collective future. And
there is a choice in the exact sense, implying that there are real
alternatives, that one has to choose to commit one's life in one
direction or another.

This is because the situation of the poor in Latin America
makes it necessary to choose between a life of effective love for
others, of service in the cause of the oppressed people, and a
quiet life, seeking one's own well-being and—if possible—
advancement in society as it exists. If the "tendency" under
discussion were something more automatic, a social pressure,
the second choice would be the norm: opting for following the
usual channels of the dominant culture and supporting the "historical purpose" of the ruling elites.

The other option, in favour of the cause of the poor, obviously
means making a definite choice to swim against the prevailing
current, a choice that has to bring personal conscience, a feeling
of responsibility for the people and their future, and one's personal freedom, deeply into play. Responsibility has to be exercised as clear-sightedly as possible with regard to actual
conditions, viable and effective means, and—often—lesser evils.
This means putting a whole process of analysis and discernment

into making this choice. Without this, particularly in the field of
political activism in situations of institutionalized violence, ide-
alistic aims and self-sacrifice—especially among young people—
can easily degenerate into an absolutizing revolutionary mystique, ready to use any means at whatever cost. The result of
this, unfortunately, is generally to serve the interests of the
oppressors and heap even more suffering on the heads of the
majority of the people. This is the lesson of the section on
"Peace" in Medellín's "Final Document." (The theological
implications of this revolutionary "temptation" are examined in
the light of the Gospels, below, in chapter VI, section 3c.)

Traditional mentality sees life and society as governed by a
law, as preordained through a series of rules or commandments,
all basically negative: "thou shalt not" do this or that; "it is
forbidden" to do the other. . . . Good behaviour, the virtuous
and orderly life, then seems to consist in not "trespassing"
beyond any set limits, in "doing no one any harm," in "not
getting involved" in anything that might cause conflict. Personal
freedom, under such a scheme of things, would lie in the possibilities for either obeying this law or rebelling against it; sooner
or later, this would bring reward for obedience, punishment for
disobedience. The new mentality I have opposed to this traditional one sees a call to freedom in life itself. It understands
freedom as liberation from oppressive conditions, as liberation
from the barriers—external or in one's own psychological make-
up—that prevent one from growing as oneself, from truly loving,
from putting the best of oneself at the service of others. It sees
freedom as liberation from our servitudes and fears, as conscious
assumption of our actual conditions of life and responsible initiative in favour of the new. This is the freedom to seek the new
and to make mistakes; freedom to risk one's life—responsibly—
in the cause of justice, with the joy and dangers such a course
of action implies.

(b) Crisis of "God"

The traditional culture we have been looking at involves not
only a concept of individual and societal life, but also one of
God. Understandably, therefore, the new experience of life as

a call to freedom, and of individual life and history as a challenge to human creativity, produces a crisis in the received image of God. To be more precise, it produces a crisis in the image of God as Law-giver, who has from the beginning laid down an established order of things hedged round with prohibitions; of God as omniscient, being everywhere to see into our most secret deeds and thoughts; of God as judge, taking note of everything and handing out rewards and punishments according to our obedience or disobedience. Most fundamentally—especially for more thoughtful people—it produces a crisis in the idea of God as Lord and master of life and history; of a predestining God, knowing, planning and determining everything from all eternity; of a God whose sovereign will and omnipotence seem to leave no space for human creative initiative and true responsibility, turning us into mere instruments, witting or unwitting, of God's unchangeable designs. It produces a crisis in the image of a God who—being beyond all appearances and contradictions—would in effect be the sole author of and only actor in the drama of human history, the only one who really "writes" history and, despite its crooked lines, carries it straight to its transcendent conclusion.

(c) New Perspectives

Once again, we can see that the crisis of the received image of God has a purifying effect, setting us free to inquire into the real nature of the biblical witness to the living God. This is above all, as we have seen in the previous sections, a witness to a God who, freely and out of love, creates genuinely free human beings.

God does not create out of any internal need; nor are human creatures pure shadows of the will of God: the God revealed in the Bible is the absolute opposite of what we might—and so often do—picture as universal organizer of the origins of the world, omnipotent eye seeing through everything, best programmed computer and perfect machine for dispensing automatic justice. Insofar as we carry such conceptions with us, just reading the Bible can be deeply disconcerting. However, it is not just the Bible (if we read it), but also life itself, individual and collective (if we live it honestly), that will make us feel ever stranger in our condition of faithful believers—or force us to keep our religious beliefs "safe" for certain occasions of life . . . or death. The challenge I wish to take up here, then, is to try to understand how we can bridge these gaps between our image of God, the Bible, and our lives. The place to begin this process is to read the Bible in all honesty and in a church community journeying with its people in a serious attempt to follow in the footsteps of Jesus Christ.

On this journey in faith, the most striking and renewing aspect of the biblical image of God is God's acting in human history as someone sovereignly free, who cannot be encapsulated in any schema or manipulated by any artifice. God visits us on our ground, coming to meet us gratuitously and completely unpredictably, as freedom personified, calling us to be free and to put our freedom radically at risk. God comes as our friend, and it is in becoming more fully ourselves and a human community that we know God. Four steps in biblical revelation, brought to life among the poor today, will illustrate this more fully:

1. First of all, the God we discover in the Bible is not simply one who exists eternally beyond all contingency, immutable beyond all change, ever the same, the one thing necessary and secure; the God of the Bible intervenes in human history—in a very concrete history with all its contingencies and uncertainties, and does so in an unpredictable and surprising way, out of spontaneous and sovereignly free love, in order to create something new. This is the living God whom we today—in the light of that same Bible—miss desperately, call on urgently and salute on meeting, in our present history as a people.

2. The God of the Bible intervenes in our history not in order to act alone and change things by working miracles; not in order to shine before us as punisher of transgressions or magical problem-solver. It is true that there are places in the Bible where God is pictured in this way. The Bible itself-as we shall see in more detail later—reflects the primitive beliefs of a people on their journey, whose faith had to be continuously purified by the blows of history and the preaching of the prophets, and, finally, radicalized by the witness of Jesus Christ.

In the light of this inner dynamic of the Bible, continued

today in our journey in faith, we see the living God intervene in history in order to arouse our reaction and commitment. God's action is a challenge addressed to us; it is a "word" seeking to set up a dialogue with us; it is "heart-to-heart" self-communication, which requires a total, radical, free and committed response from us:

> Listen, Israel: Yahweh, our God, is One Yahweh. And you shall love Yahweh, your God, with all your heart, with all your soul and with all your strength. . . . Do not forget Yahweh who took you out from Egypt where you were enslaved. . . . Do not go after other gods; do not serve any of the gods of the nations around you, because your God, who is in your midst, is a jealous God [Deut. 6:4–15].

Jesus will recognize this as "the first commandment, and the most important," adding, as inseparable from it, "another one very similar to it: You shall love your neighbour as yourself," and declaring: "The whole Law and the Prophets are founded on these two commandments" (Matt. 22:37–40; Mark 12:28–34). As a riposte to the formalistic legalism of the teachers of the Law and the Pharisees, Jesus calls us to put these two commandments into practice in sincerity of heart; to be radical in essentials — "justice, mercy and faith" — and flexible in secondary matters; to respond to specific situations by a creative practice of service (Matt. 22:34 – 23:32; Luke 10:25–37). Such is Jesus' verbal teaching, which is nothing other than the "reason" he puts forward for his own basic actions and his practice, as a free man before God, as Son, as servant freely bestowed — and with what astounding creativity! — on the neighbour in need and on "the multitude."

3. God's action in history is not that of a totalitarian power, at once distant and irresistible, watching the "play" of an inconsequential freedom with a supercilious smile. No, the God of the Bible is shown becoming truly involved in our history, seriously taking the part of oppressed individuals and people. This serious and total involvement is seen throughout biblical history, but most radically and astonishingly in that "when the fullness of time came, God sent his Son. He came born of woman and

subject to the Law ... to make us adopted sons and daughters of God" (Gal. 4:4–5). God does not look for a mechanical response from human creatures, as though they were puppets on strings; God does not look either for blind submission out of fear of punishment, as though they were slaves; what God looks for is a serious and "heartfelt" response, as from sons and daughters, from children who grow in maturity of creative freedom and intelligent commitment.

God plays a serious part and takes our response or lack of it seriously. This means that the future course of events really depends on how we — as individuals, groups, peoples — react or fail to react to God's challenge. Our freedom is real, with real consequences, and all the risks such freedom implies: of lack of response, out of indifference or hard-heartedness, because we are "serving other gods"; of tepid replies, lacking depth, half-hearted through self-interest or fear (see Matt. 6:24–34; 13:1–23). These bring about the frustration of hopes, injustices, violence and miseries of all sorts; beyond history, they lead to the final perdition of those who remain totally closed to the call of the God of life and love. The living God wants us to have life, but human life, in the image of the God who creates and gives from love. And the love worthy of the name is free, springs from "the heart" and commits itself, excluding fear and coercion (see 1 John 3:16–18), which in turn means that it involves the — tremendous — risks just described. The God of life undoubtedly prefers to take these risks rather than abuse the freedom of creatures and devalue love.

4. In any case, however closed we are to the call of generous love, however corrupted our freedom, however deep the degradation of a society through its idolatry of money, facile pleasure or despotic power ..., it is always possible that a change in the course of history will bring people and groups of people to their senses and make them "cry to the Lord" with sincerity (as is seen happening in the theological schema shown in "Deuteronomist history," embracing the books of Deuteronomy, Joshua, Judges, Samuel and Kings); it is always possible for the God of the promise — without doing us violence — to inspire conversion and a change of conduct; God's last word to us is always mercy.

It is just in this that the power and sovereign freedom of the God of life shine most strongly.[4]

The liberator God of the historical traditions and prophets of Israel is demanding and "jealous" with the chosen people, but equally faithful despite all their infidelities, to the point of promising the miracle of replacing their hearts of stone with hearts of flesh that are capable of responding in true love (see Hos. 2; Jer. 31:31–4; Exod. 36:22–30). Jesus' gospel brings "woes" and lamentations to the rich and those who have their fill, to the Pharisees who burden people's consciences, to the proud cities that fail to recognize the signs of the coming Kingdom (see Luke 6:24–6; 19:41–4; Matt. 11:20–24; 23:13–39); his God, nevertheless, is the shepherd who goes out to look for the one lost sheep, the Father who rushes out to welcome the prodigal son (see Luke 15). This is the God who seems to wait for us, waiting until, through true conversion, we open ourselves to God's great joy: that of forgiving utterly, opening the way to newness of life, to the new city "adorned as a bride prepared for her husband" (Rev. 21:2).

Here, once again, it is Jesus' practice that provides us with the key. He himself belonged to the world of the "little" people, despised by the religious elites as cursed and ignorant of the Law (see Mark 6:1–6; Luke 18:9–14; John 8:45–9; 9:13–16); he mingled with public sinners and social outcasts, prostitutes and publicans, openly welcoming them and eating with them (see Mark 2:15–17; Luke 7:36–50; 15:1ff; John 8:1–11); but he did not refuse to go into the houses of the oppressors; rather he sought to give them the opportunity of conversion: he accepted the invitation of leading Pharisees, invited himself to eat with a prominent publican, was prepared to go to the house of a Roman centurion (see Luke 7:1–10, 36–50; 11:37ff; 14:1ff; 19:1–10). These were all representatives of privileged groups, "well-off," "decent" people, representing "values" and social structures opposed to Jesus' purpose; they belonged to groups that were to become ever more openly and effectively his enemies, to the point of persecuting and getting rid of him by the most deceitful and cruel means. Jesus was very clear and strong in his public denunciation of such groups, of their real interests and their actions. But he never ceased actively seeking their conversion and redemption—because he loved them too—to the extreme of his "Father, forgive them . . ." from the cross.

It is this practice of Jesus', going to this extreme, that shows the most radical face of God's committed freedom in dealing with us, the deepest and most irrevocable choice made by the God who relates to human creatures on an intensely personal level: love (see Rom. 3:21–6; 5:1–11; 8:31–9; John 3:14–17; 12:20–32; 1 John 4:7–16). And by the same token, this provides the basic touchstone—that is, forgiving and loving our enemies—for those who follow Jesus, who believe in the God and Father Jesus showed us. This forgiveness and love of enemies is how we witness most radically to our trust in God's love for us, and in our freedom as human beings (see Matt. 5:20–26, 38–48; 6:12–15; 18:21–35; Luke 6:27–38; 15:25–32; 1 John 4:7–16).

3. GOD IN THE LIFE AND DEATH OF THE OPPRESSED

The two preceding sections have shown that the God of the Bible and of our journey in faith is the God of life; that this God awakens and calls forth our active responsibility in the situation and time we live in; that God's last word to us, as individuals and peoples, is mercy. The previous chapter dealt first with the creator God, in relation to human life and death as "natural" processes, bound up with the world of nature, and then with the liberator God in relation to social oppression and the responding solidarity of the oppressed people. I should now like to take the "reflection from our situation" a last step forward by examining the experience of God found in the life and death of this oppressed people.

I propose to do this by drawing specifically on the experience of God found in the base communities in Chile. Not too long ago, three hundred representatives from base church communities came together in Santiago to share and reflect on their experiences. The theme of the meeting was "the face of God," God as found in our living faith, the God of our life and suffering as an oppressed people and of our commitment in solidarity, seen in the light of our Christian faith.

Some of the ground will inevitably have been covered in preceding sections, but I hope the material will be shown in a new

light here, and brought closer to our actual experience of faith.
More specifically, I hope that the faith of our simpler brothers
and sisters, speaking in their own words, will guide us in this
darkest and most daring passage in our reflection, because it is
just in this area, that of the unjust suffering and violent death
of the oppressed, that the radical limitation of all theological
discourse has been most in evidence.

(a) Witness

When simple Christians tackle the subject of God, one of the
first observations to surface is usually that "it is in the communities that we find the living God." This is because – they say –
"if we are trying to live as Christians, we absorb the word of
God in what we do . . . and then we have to be seeing God in
people, in the children, the unemployed, the outcasts . . ."; and
it is because "we know Christ better in the communities, and
then what people suffer matters. . . . It throws light on what we
see, and then we take people's suffering as our responsibility,
with more eagerness." And the fact is that God "acts among us
by calling us into communities, and there lifts us up and encour-
ages us, and sends us out with new strength to live and struggle."

1. When we ask who God is in the situation we live in, the
first answers that come up – with the strength of a new conviction, but one now deeply rooted – are negative: the oppressive
situation we are in "can't be attributed to God." "Unemployment and poverty, the fact that we can't do anything . . . are the
product of an unjust structure, not God's will; the fear and insecurity we suffer from are the product of a repressive dictatorship, not God. God doesn't want this and doesn't do it." The
cause of so much deprivation, so much suffering and cruelty, "is
not God, but men, social sin, the way things are organized."
What we find here is an "absence" of God; we find a God
"silenced by this oppression"; we discover that "this situation is
itself sin," offence to and rejection of God.

This is the new reaction to the idea deeply rooted in many
people, particularly the older ones: that the situation "comes
from God," that we are suffering because God is punishing us
("What can we have done for God to punish us like this?").

This is an image of a God who does not liberate but stifles, the image of a "dictator God." And this religious oppression, which imposes conformism, is now seen as "worse than the dictatorship itself."

People understand that the Bible itself provides many words and images that give this impression of God. So this gives rise to the questions: "How do we read the Bible in the right way, to discover a liberating God? How can we do this when many people read the Bible in all sorts of ways, and even use it to justify oppression?" And the poor give their verdict: "The church and the priests are largely to blame for people not knowing the Bible, . . . for making them worship God by beating their breasts. The priests kept the Bible to themselves; the church made it taboo." The way to finding an answer is clear: "The key is Jesus Christ: who he is and how he acts. He never oppressed anyone; on the contrary, he was one of the oppressed." "The Bible lends itself to different interpretations . . . but we have to read it from Jesus' viewpoint, as he understood it." "If we read the Bible together in community, we are doing that: reading it from Christ's viewpoint. We're shaking the dust off it when we read it together." "Before, the church was distant; it was the priests. Now the church is here; it's us: all together, all responsible."

2. So for our brothers and sisters in the base communities, God is not "above" the poor people, imposing their state of destitution and death on them, as the upper classes, the government and the military are above them. On the contrary — and this is the source of the great "good news" for the people — God is "in" the very history of the oppressed: "God is truly incarnate in the people, in their personal and collective experiences"; "God is the one most affected by the situation" from which the people suffer; God is "present in their passion and weeping." God is not in the rich with their feasting, nor in Herod, but in the poor man lying under the table, in the persecuted child forced into exile with his parents. The living God — the only true one — is not on the side of the dictator and his "security forces" who kill and lie, nor with the financial groups who need all this security apparatus and support it for the sake of their sacred "free market." God is with the people, oppressed and stripped

of their means of livelihood, with those who are tortured, with the "troublemakers" who are taken away and slaughtered in the night.

3. We find God present in the poor people, suffering with the oppressed. This experience of "God-with-us," however, is not just one of shared suffering: the God who is and suffers with the oppressed is the God of life, the liberator God. This is why God is with those deprived of a life of human dignity, with those threatened with violent death, with the imprisoned. God is with them not only to enable them to "hang on" in the situation they are enduring; God is there "judging that situation," "summoning" the oppressed themselves to take cognizance of the injustice and to "commit themselves to changing the state of affairs." This is the God who "walks with," but who also "awakens and summons," who "sends us out with new strength for the journey and the struggle."

God, then, is revealed even to the oppressed people as their liberator. This liberation, however, does not fall from above, either directly from heaven or through the ruling classes or messianic organizations. God is, in Christ, incarnate in the lives and collective history of the oppressed themselves, working from within the people, their own organizations, communities and hearts, infusing courage, cohesion and clarity through the Holy Spirit, working for a new life and a new society, so that "we can change the oppressive state of affairs" and build a society of solidarity and justice.

4. So the liberator God is in the oppressed people giving them strength, and this presence is a summons, a challenge to the people as a whole and to each individual. This is where God's call is heard: "in historical situations, inviting us and presenting us with an alternative way of life, with a purpose. . . ." "God does not will this situation, which is social sin, but wants us to sort it out ourselves." "God is inviting us to build the Kingdom, here and now, by transforming this world." "The hope and strength God gives us are not just to hold on, but to accomplish this task, and to do it with courage and joy." "In the past, we were told we just had to be patient, but really we are being told we have to act . . . and it is God who is telling us this." "It matters to know that God is with us, but also that God is there to

make us build the Kingdom . . ., showing real alternatives to a frustrated and downtrodden people."

"Some respond and others don't" to this invitation. "Generally speaking, those who do are the poor, because they're more available." But among the poor too, "some respond and some don't." If we don't respond, if we "hang back," we are "accomplices in social sin"; we too "are guilty of perpetuating this regime," through not agitating, through letting ourselves be dominated by fear or egoism. "If we don't respond, God leaves us; but if we turn back to God with a will to respond, God gives us strength, like with the prodigal son."

5. We have to recognize the God of life, the liberator God, in "signs of the Kingdom among the poor": solidarity, consciousness, commitment. This is the "God of life and solidarity" who is present and active in "organizations working for change," "in those who give their lives for the people." So we find a "liberator Christ in the poor," more in their actions than in their words; we see "the Spirit in the people," "awakening them, summoning them to conversion and commitment," encouraging and "strengthening the weak to struggle against the tremendous power of social sin," of injustice and institutionalized violence.

In this sense too, the God of life sends us out, fortified by the Spirit, as Christians and Christian communities, to make the liberator God known to our brothers and sisters of the people. Faced with their image of a God who punishes and oppresses, "our mission is to make known the liberator God, the only true one, who does not want us oppressed." It is our practice, our approach, that can make this God known: "If we show this courage and strength in the midst of suffering and struggle, many people will ask: Where do they get this strength from?" And we have to show this God present in the people themselves, "when they share from their poverty, when they take risks and give themselves for their friends."

Such, then, is the verbal witness provided by our brothers and sisters from the communities, Christians from the oppressed people and from the church, in their meeting to discuss "the face of God."

(b) Reflection

1. Christ, the Messiah of God, who shows his true face and love given for us, is the persecuted and crucified Christ who

continues his passion in the oppressed of the world and all those crucified throughout history. At the same time, he is the risen Christ, who overcomes unjust suffering and violent death; who liberates us from all oppressions; who is Lord of life and all truly human community, the firstborn of many brothers and sisters in the full joy of the Father and of the Kingdom.

The first dimension, Christ as the crucified one, has sunk deep roots in the religious faith of our simple people, roots going back to the first evangelization of the continent and the earliest prophetic witnesses to the "scourged Christs of the Indies." The oppressed people see themselves in the images of Christ mocked and wounded. In the traditional faith of the people, the image of the cross and the celebration of Good Friday occupy a central place, bringing back the Christian memory—so expressive and important to the poor—of departed loved ones and especially those who have been victims of violent death.

The second dimension, Christ as the risen one, has come to occupy a more important place with renewed evangelization of the religious faith and life of the people, in and around the base communities. This evangelization is discovering and encouraging signs of new life and seeds of hope in the journey the people are making: signs of increased consciousness and dignity, new areas of community spirit and popular cultural expression, seeds of local organization and collective liberation.

This new consciousness brought to the people in communities by the light of the gospel has also produced a new approach to the image of Christ crucified, one that connects more closely with the second dimension, of the risen Christ, as this has been rediscovered. This is a more historical approach to conflict in society: Jesus suffered and died on the scaffold of the cross not because "it was written," not because it was the direct "will of God." He suffered and died because he remained faithful to the end to the mission entrusted to him, in a society dominated by the power of sin. In a society ruled by idolatry of money, the pomp of governors, a formalistic and corrupted "religious observance," it was logical and foreseeable that Jesus' proclamation of the Kingdom to the poor, his liberating practice toward the oppressed, and his "programme" as set out in the beatitudes would come into mortal conflict with the dominant "values" and the groups who held power. They were the ones who persecuted, condemned and executed Jesus, the anointed one of God.

By contrast with the religious ideology of sacrifice or the theological theory of expiatory suffering, the faith of the communities does not see sin in the crucified Christ, does not see him taking the place of sinners to suffer and make reparation "for" them. On the contrary, sin is seen, in all its death-dealing and deceiving power, in those who crucified him.[5] The oppressors of the weak, those who commit deicide, are the instruments of sin, not of God!

The God of life—the God of the Kingdom, Father of Jesus Christ—is not seen as active in the passion and death of Christ, but in the resurrection. On the cross, God is rather absent, rejected: absent at least as powerful God, though present suffering with and in the crucified Jesus, so seen as God repressed, tortured even to death. God in full power appears as the God who raises Jesus, the anointed and beloved Son, crucified by the rulers of the world; as the God who justifies the one unjustly condemned, who raises and gives glorious and wonderfully fruitful life to the one the oppressors executed with such cruelty, trying to remove all trace of him from the face of the earth. And this is exactly how the early Christians experienced and proclaimed the power of God—and they were an oppressed people like ours. It is also the nucleus of apostolic preaching, as found in Acts and the letters of St Paul.[6]

So our brothers and sisters in the communities can say (returning to their witness given at that meeting): "God is always with us, and especially in the most difficult situations. . . . These are where we feel God inspiring us and keeping us together, in service and giving." "When we are beaten and thrown out, we remember the example of Christ being rejected, and take heart." This is why those church communities most directly affected by repression of the church have, with the Spirit of the risen Christ, carried on the rich Christian tradition of bearing persecution and martyrdom, the evangelical tradition illuminated and deepened by pastors such as Oscar Romero and Enrique Alvear in recent years of dictatorship and repression. To go back to our witnesses once more:

> Yesterday, God was with Ricardo in the torture
> chamber,

and yesterday his companion in torture was
  Jesus Christ.
And Ricardo's companion said:
It was the other one who was alone,
the one who placed the electrodes,
who carried out the torture,
who threatened with his revolver
and went on and on with the questions . . .
I don't know how to say it, said Ricardo,
but I know that God was with me and is life,
and I think: How lonely to be a torturer!

So beyond the deaths of those persecuted and assassinated
"for justice' sake," their words resound among the people —
words like those above; words like these: "If they kill me, I shall
rise again in the Salvadorean people," spoken by Archbishop
Romero in an interview given just a few weeks before his death;
or these, written on posters in Chile when Fr Andrés Jarlan was
killed: "You will rise again in the people's struggle." Their words
resound because these are our confessors and martyrs today;
these, on the journey of our oppressed people, are the great
witnesses to the risen Christ and the God of life.

2. To give this testimony to the God of the oppressed its full
evangelical weight, suffice to contrast it with "the problem of
evil" and of the suffering of the innocent as it is usually posed
in Western theology, with the images of God it implies and
which are often transmitted in preaching.

Since the beginning of Christianity, its detractors have
pointed to the "dead ends" to which the Christian doctrine of
God leads when faced with the evil in the world, the tremendous
power of injustice and violence throughout history, which is
apparently without compensation or hope. If all this exists — they
say — it must be for one of three reasons: (a) because God actually wills it or at least positively allows it; (b) because God is
way above all such things and is not concerned with them; or
(c) because God is unable to prevent such things.[7] Or, we can
add from a modern standpoint, simply because God does not
exist. These options sum up the whole problem of the "theodicy"
or philosophical justification of God that has so influenced eccle-

siastical preaching and Christian teaching over the centuries.

(a) By stressing primarily the power of an irresistible God present in all things, and insisting that God wills or positively allows the evil in the world, we are producing an image of a punishing God, and even of an angry, cruel God. We then look for a theodicy of a juridical or penal nature, leading to the image of God as judge, who "must" hand down sentences according to a positive law, automatically; or of God as banker, crediting and debiting our account on a cosmic computer. This image feeds into a pious and ritualistic mystique of expiatory suffering and sacrifice, in turn producing an image of a jealous God, even a violent and bloodthirsty God, whose anger "demands" the suffering and expiatory death of God's creature. The Old Testament itself — as fundamentalist readings of it today still show — can be used to support such an understanding of God, if approached ahistorically and not from a proper Christian standpoint.[8]

Now the suffering people themselves give the lie to all this. Reflecting in communities, they calmly and joyously see that such images do not correspond to their own experience of the gospel among the oppressed; they find such images more appropriate to the "god" who is on the side of the ruling powers with their institutionalized violence, to the caricature of the Christian God often trotted out by the authorities and used in their self-justifying rites.

(b) By stressing primarily God's transcendence and infinite distance above our material world and its troubles, we are saying that, basically, God is unaffected by all this, and are thereby proposing the experience and image of a distant, even indifferent and cynical God. We then look for a metaphysical type of theodicy: one derived from Greek philosophy, opposing perfection of being to all historical evolution, purity of act to all passion. This produces the image of an impassive God, unchanging in perfection of being and self-sufficiency, a mystery unattainable to mortals with their bodily sufferings and historical trials. This feeds into a religious mysticism of the "ascent of the soul," an asceticism of self-control of all passions in quest of unchanging perfection and even of indifference.[9] This is the "way" found in much of the spiritual literature — old and new — that we priests and religious read in our seminaries and convents.

Now we priests and religious, journeying together and reading the Bible together with the oppressed, are finding that this spirituality and image of God do not fit the lasting experience of the humble people of God, do not fit the living God of the scriptures, the Father of Jesus Christ; rather we are finding that this spirituality and image of God belong to the impassive Infinite Being of Greek religious philosophy. We are seeing that this image of God reflects the experience and aims of the bourgeoisie, of the historical subjects of the modern "Christian West," who live, justify and impose the civilization of egoism, found at its most extreme in the islands of prosperity in the Third World, where elite minorities cultivate their personal development, human perfection and peace behind huge ramparts of willful ignorance and cynicism thrown up to keep out the vast ocean of poverty and oppression that surrounds them — and sustains them.[10]

(c) The third alternative, that God cannot prevent the injustice and violence in the world, comes closer to the experience of the oppressed people. I say "closer" since the other two options — that an almighty God wills or permits the evil in the world, or that a transcendent God is above it all — also point very distantly and very partially toward the mystery of God. And because here too, by saying that God "cannot" prevent it, we are very partially evoking a mystery that indeed passes our understanding.

The two statements — "God is almighty" and "God cannot prevent so much unjust suffering" — can of course be seen as simply contradictory. This is true if we "place" God outside history; if, on the other hand — in the light of the gospel and the testimony adduced — we see God involved with the oppressed and the crucified of history; if we see God combatting, out of love, evil and injustice where they hurt most . . . then the contradiction and scandal are turned into mystery. Then it is no longer we who question God about evil and injustice, but God — voluntarily crucified in Jesus and the crucified of history — who questions and challenges us. Then it is no longer we who have to "justify" God (theodicy), but the very God who has to justify us (as with St Paul — see Rom. 3:21–6; 5:1–11), accomplices that we are, through action or passivity, in the sin of the world that oppresses and slaughters the wretched of the earth.

If God really wills the autonomy of the created world through its own dynamic, if God really takes human freedom seriously (see section 2, above), then God "cannot" prevent all the unjust suffering. More specifically, historically, God "cannot" prevent all this if God's love is found in identification in solidarity with the oppressed of the earth, if God has chosen to take on the poverty and powerlessness of the poor so as to be, from within these, the spirit and power of the Kingdom and its justice.

With regard to the fourth option mentioned—that God does not exist—I would simply say here that from the standpoint of the poor and more specifically the Christian poor, atheism fails to resolve the problem of unjust evil in the world; that the reverse is true: that believing with the oppressed in the God of Jesus Christ gives meaning and strength to go on living and struggling together.

PART THREE

BIBLICAL REFLECTION

INTRODUCTION

Biblical Revelation and Our Experience of God

1. WHERE AND HOW WE READ THE BIBLE

The journey in faith described in part 1, undertaken in the social setting of the poor majority of the people, is uncovering dimensions of the biblical message that had been overlaid by the way we understood and lived our faith till a few years ago. Really, as John Paul II said in Brazil: "In different concrete settings, the church re-reads these texts and scrutinizes these messages [about its origins] so as to find a new application in them." So the fact of the growing consciousness of solidarity among a believing people suffering marginalization and injustice, the fact that more and more Christians from the base communities are taking part in popular movements for social liberation, the fact that the church itself is beginning to recognize the tradition of a workers' movement that sprang up outside it and has till recently kept apart from ecclesiastical circles – all this has led us to what has become known as "the option for the poor."

The God of Jesus Christ is the universal saviour of all humankind – saviour, however, of all in their history, from their particular place in society. The biblical tradition shows the history of Israel's development of a progressively clearer image of God as truly universal and as the only creator and saviour of all

peoples and all human beings. But specifically, in the historical
actions recognized by the faith of the prophets, God is always
seen as the liberator of the exploited, the avenger of the
oppressed, the guarantor of justice and right for widows and
orphans, workers and strangers; God is always shown as the God
of an oppressed people, and of the different categories of poor
and outcasts thrown up by the changing historical situation of
that people.

This is seen even more clearly in Jesus' preaching and messianic activity: God is the universal Father who "makes the sun
to shine on sinners and on just," but the coming of God's Reign
to this world of sin and oppression is good news to the poor,
since the God of the Kingdom comes in solidarity with the outcasts and oppressed of that particular society in which Jesus
lived, comes to change things in their favour. There are several
passages in the Gospels that contain a programmatic summary
of Jesus' messianic activity, and show this "social partiality" of
God in provocative and even—for us—scandalous form: there
is Jesus' opening speech in the synagogue at Nazareth in Luke
4; his reply to the disciples of John the Baptist in Luke 7 and
Matthew 11; there are the beatitudes in Matthew 5 and Luke
6, and the praise given to the Father for revealing "these things"
to simple people in Matthew 11 and Luke 10. The same applies
to Mary's Magnificat in Luke 1, which takes words from the
Psalms to hymn the God who "has put down the mighty from
their thrones and lifted up those who are downtrodden," who
"has filled the hungry with good things but has sent the rich
away empty." These are all strong words, paradoxical ones for
us, which Jesus put into effect in his actions and which proved
highly conflictive in his social setting.

This is a historical-social dimension of the gospel which had
not been strongly present in the received understanding of our
faith, and which therefore burst upon the church in Latin America with renewing strength. Picked out and elaborated on by
liberation theology, it was taken up at the Medellín Conference,
which spoke of the "poverty of the church," and again at Puebla,
which defined the "option for the poor."

The liberation, new life and new social order brought by Jesus
to the poor of the earth, and, from the poor, to all those disposed

to be converted to them, have a definite content. The Reign Jesus proclaimed and inaugurated implies a dynamism of integral human liberation—meaning that the good news brought by Jesus concerns the whole human being and all dimensions of human life. It is not just a revindication of spiritual or religious values, or a message of hope for beyond death. It contains these, and they are fundamental to it, but it is devalued when separated from Jesus' liberating action, from a gift of the God of life, directed to us in our totality and committing us completely. The good news of salvation, the Reign of God or will of the Father, apply equally to our spiritual calling and to our material needs, to us as individuals and in communities, to our lives and society on this earth and to the life and "city" to come. This is why those of us who are not poor find it easy to "defend ourselves" from this good news, telling ourselves that the poverty God seeks is "spiritual poverty" and that the "materially poor" will be rewarded in the next life. The fortunate destiny of the poor Lazarus is true, but so is the terrible fate of those who eat well without worrying about the "material" needs of their fellow men and women (Luke 16). And we have been warned in our own days that the "contrasts" and "confrontation" found in the world of today "represent, as it were, the gigantic growth of the biblical parable of the rich man and Lazarus" (RH 16).

"Experience of God" is a basic theme that has come to the fore in recent years. The form of experience we are dealing with here arises from our objective experience of massive poverty and injustice, and from the commitment to the liberative struggle made by growing sections of the Christian community. This situation and commitment in solidarity, experienced by individual Christians and church communities, incorporate growing recognition of and obedience to the God of Jesus Christ; they involve—as we have seen—perception of the liberating presence, and the rejection, of the living God, perception of ways to follow Jesus in practice, and understanding of the ways we can remain shut into our old certainties and fatalism; they produce a "spiritual experience," a "spirituality," in the best Christian sense of these words.

Knowledge of God therefore comes to us here on the level of experience and history. This is a God who is sensed and

"known" in our lives and the course of our history: in, that is,
the journey we undertake with the oppressed people and the
Christian community that travels alongside them; in situations
we face together, our commitment to solidarity with the people,
the experiences we undergo with them. This is not something
new in Christianity: we are simply rediscovering and re-evaluating the old tradition of a God seen at work in the collective
history of the human race, a God we recognize in the prophetic
word we find acting on us and calling us on our own journey as
a people. This is the same God who acted "of old" with "the
fathers" and whose liberative action reached its fullness in Jesus
Christ, the same God who is constantly acting on us and challenging us to respond in the here and now of our own history,
the same God who opens up the future to us and inspires us
with the certain hope of the Kingdom to come.

Clearly, our history and liberative practice do not necessarily
or automatically produce this experience of God. Human life
and history are in themselves ambiguous: they do not in themselves "speak" to us of God and God's liberative action; they
do so only in the light of a prophetic word which we recognize
as inspired by this same God of history. It is only in the light of
faith, rooted in the living tradition of the biblical word, that
history undergone and liberating practice speak to us of God,
themselves become "experience" of God. For us, this implies
re-evaluating and reinterpreting two very central aspects of all
Christian spirituality: contemplation and the practical search for
God's will. We need a contemplation that seeks to discern the
signs and follow the traces of the presence or absence of God,
God's liberating action or its rejection, in the daily lives of individuals and the history of the people. This is needed not only
to recognize and praise God in liturgical worship, but for a
"knowledge" that implies allowing oneself to become involved
and to commit oneself: an experience bound up in the active
search for the Father's will, in the active following of Christ.

Two essential conditions are required for this: contemplative
attention to life and history, and the community of believers
historically committed to its own message of liberation. This
contemplative attention implies openness to the Spirit, permanent discernment, a constant effort to purify the eye of faith;

this community of believers makes a "situated" reading of the word of scripture, and is called together to celebrate and proclaim the faith in consciousness of the actively responsible part it has to play in the history of God's liberating actions. So, the church community is properly the place where this contemplative attention is gathered and formulated, and where this reading of the biblical word that deciphers and reinforces our experience of God is done.

2. THE ONE GOD OF THE BIBLE AND WORLD RELIGIONS

(a) The Origins of the Religion of the Bible

The Bible begins God's revelation to the chosen people with Abraham; here is the first link between "revealed religion" and nature religions. The existence of "patriarchs" is confirmed by archeology, which has found names, customs and institutions that belong to the biblical "legends" of the patriarchs and that do not reappear later in Israel's history. To the question of what exactly the religion of the patriarchs might have been, other than its re-reading in later Israel, historians of religion have given various replies:

1. Following Gressmann,[1] some authors stress the fact that the patriarchs appear at different stages of their wanderings worshipping God under different names. So they would establish a cult of "God Most High" (Gen. 14:17ff), or "God Almighty" (Gen. 17:1–2), in relation always to a sacred place or object – a tree, a stone, a well. In each of these places, the patriarchs would have paid homage to the god worshipped there by the local Canaanites. It was only later that the various names came to be considered attributes of the one same God.

2. Others, following Alt,[2] without denying the truth of this, hold that when they came to Canaan, the patriarchs brought their own religion with them. As normal with nomadic peoples, this would not be tied to particular places, but to the clan or tribe, with special reference to revered ancestral figures. This is how they interpret the texts that designate the divinity in relation to the various "fathers" (see Gen. 26:24ff; 28:11ff; 31; 49:24;

also Exod. 3:1–6). So the "God of Abraham," the "Fearful God of Isaac" and the "Mighty One of Jacob" would all be different divinities, later brought together in the monotheistic tradition of Israel.

3. The excavations at Ugarit (1929 on) have shown that throughout the Syro-Canaanite world, there was a pantheon of similar gods worshipped above the local deities, and that the supreme God of this pantheon was El, creator and lord of heaven and earth and also of the other gods. Linguistically, "El" does not just mean an individual of the genus "elín" (gods), but was the proper name of the supreme God. Accordingly, in Genesis 21:33, for example, "El 'Olam" should not be translated as "Yahweh, the everlasting God" (as in most modern translations), nor as "the god Eternity" (Gressmann), but "El, the everlasting one." This would not, then, be a local divinity of Beer-sheba, but the supreme and creator God, known throughout Canaan as "El" and here worshipped with the epithet "everlasting."

On the other hand, it is not possible to conclude simply that the patriarchs came to know the cult of El, with his different epithets and sanctuaries, only when they came to the West Bank of the Jordan, since the creator God El was also known in the north, and in Mesopotamia there was a God who was creator and king of gods, whom the patriarchs could easily have identified with the El of the Canaanite cult. Furthermore, designation of a divinity by reference to an ancestor is not confined to nomadic cultures. Rural and urban polytheism also frequently invokes one of its gods as special protector of a family and defines this god in relation to its ancestors. So the Bible too does not always refer to the God of the fathers without a name: besides the (late) designation "Yahweh," there are passages in which he is called "El, God of Israel" (Gen. 33:20), "El, God of your father" (Gen. 46:3) and the like.

We can accept Lohfink's conclusion:

The patriarchs and their descendants worshipped the creator god El, known throughout Canaan, and regarded him as the one God among all gods with whom, as family god, the whole clan had a special relationship. They regarded

him in this way because they were convinced that this God
had revealed himself to the forebears of the family ...
[giving them the mandate to emigrate to the south of
Canaan and the promise of numerous descendants and the
conquest of the country]. The patriarchs, then, had what
we would call "mystical experiences." But in these they
saw clearly that God who was now being revealed to them
was a god they already knew, ... whom they had worshipped under the name of El as king of gods and all
creatures, as creator of heaven and earth. ... But now they
were tied to him in a new way, since he had returned to
them, revealed himself to them and opened the future to
them with his promises.[3]

When it incorporated the legends of the religion of the patriarchs into the Pentateuch, Mosaic Yahwism did not reject the
polytheism of the fathers, but assimilated it as the prelude to
and pre-history of Yahwism itself. By doing so, it made primitive
ritual actions and mythical sources flow into faith in the God of
Israel. This assimilation was interpreted theologically by assign-
ing ever wider scope to the religious origins of Israel, finally
reaching the priestly theology of the covenant of Yahweh/Elo-
him with Noah and, in him, all humanity and living things. The
more particular covenants God made—with Abraham, Moses
and David—are then shown against the backdrop of this universal covenant. Through this same process, the properly polytheistic element and the competition from other gods were
eliminated by subjecting all other gods and foreign powers to
the one genuinely divine power: that of Yahweh. The rest were
either demoted to Yahweh's army or council, or totally nullified
(Isa. 40–55).
   Referring to this as a "process" does not, of course, suggest
that it was a "history of ideas" or "development of doctrine" of
the sort we know. The determining factor would rather have
been the historical experiences and collective memory of the
people, re-lived and re-read in the light of the preaching of the
prophets. First and foremost was the experience of the exile,
which forced the people to re-read the whole of their earlier
history—with their theology of the special covenant with Yah-

weh their God—on a universal plane, that of the sovereign
power and salvific design of Yahweh himself for all nations and
the whole of creation. Historically, this period marks the birth
of unequivocal acceptance of the creator God and the emphatic
monotheism of Second Isaiah (40–55): "Am I not Yahweh?
There is no other God besides Me, a Saviour, a God of justice"
(Isa. 45:21; see also 40:12–29; 41:21–4; 42:5–8; 43:8–12; 44:6–8,
24–8; 45:1–25; 48:12–16; 51:12–13; 54:4–5). This is the definitive
step from monolatry (worshipping one of the gods alone, and
forbidding worship of "foreign gods") to monotheism (proclaiming one God alone, the only one that exists).

When Israel, under Solomon, became an international power,
it began to assimilate the practical wisdom of the palace scribes
of Egypt and other neighbouring kingdoms. This process continued throughout the whole period of monarchy and exile, producing—in Proverbs, Ecclesiasticus, Ecclesiastes and the Book
of Job—lessons in "wisdom in life" on a general ethical and
religious level, in which historical worship of Yahweh took second place. Here too, however, there is a process of assimilation,
with its corresponding theological interpretation, re-reading the
earlier tradition. This is achieved through the hypostasizing of
"Wisdom," who has been with God since he created the heavens
and the earth, and who is now revealed to all those who seek
her. This same Wisdom is seen as revealed in a special way in
the history of Israel, inspiring its prophets, and is seen most
particularly in the Mosaic Law (see Prov. 1–9; Ecclus. 1:1–20;
24; 42:15–50:24; Bar. 3:9–4:4).

In the Hellenistic period, and above all in the Jewish communities of the diaspora, the ancient wisdom of the East—and
the whole Bible—had to be translated into the concepts and
images of the popular religious philosophy of the Greek world.
This produced the Septuagint version, the Book of Wisdom, and
several passages in the New Testament whose theology seems
to be influenced—at least indirectly—by Philo and other Hellenistic Jews.

These strata of the Bible show more clearly than ever how
"natural knowledge of God" goes on being the basis of revealed
biblical religion: how faith in the God of Abraham, of Israel, of
Jesus Christ, is based on faith in God the creator who reveals

the divine self to and saves all those who seek God; this is the faith that the encounter with the God of the biblical tradition makes more concrete, purifies and intensifies (see Wisd. of Sol. 1:1–3, 12; 13–14; Acts 17:22–3; Rom. 1:19–21; John 1:1–14).

While this may be clear from the viewpoint of the history of religions or "fundamental theology," on the actual historical level where the faith of Israel and the Christian faith are experienced, however, their witness always involves confrontation with strange gods or the empty idols of those who "know not" the living God. This confrontation unmasks them as gods of oppression and death, as vain idols and instruments of the social lie "of those who have silenced the truth by their ways" (Rom. 1:18). This produced Israel's zeal for uncontaminated fidelity to the God of the covenant, and Jewish and Christian missions to other peoples, with the pressing call to "turn from idols to the . . . living and true God" (1 Thess. 1:9; cf. Deut. 17:14–20; 1 Kings 11:4–13; 12:12–15; 21:26; 2 Kings 21:1–18).

(b) Greek Conception of the Divine and Biblical Experience

The subject of the parallel and confrontation between the biblical experience of God and the religious thinking of Hellenism needs a section to itself. Its importance for us derives from the fact that this was the religious thinking that the first Christian missions, those of the Apostles and their followers who composed the New Testament, found in the world around them. So "Greek conception of the divine" here means, in very general terms, the philosophical-religious system of beliefs and thought prevailing in the Eastern Greco-Roman world at the time of the Judeo-Hellenistic diaspora and the first expansion of Christianity.

In this cultural setting, "Theos" did not suggest oneness of being, but oneness of a divine world: the organic and structured unity of the religious universe, which was essentially polytheistic. This plurality of the divine world persisted in Greek thought, in one form or another, to its end, despite numerous attempts to reduce the philosophical concept of God to oneness, stripped of all anthropomorphism. For the Greeks, this plurality expressed the richness of the divine, with the gods each personifying basic aspects of the world—polyfaceted aspects, which often crossed and clashed in human hearts. Faced with the deep, splendid and varied reality displayed by the cosmos, the Greeks asserted that this—and not the "utterly other"—was God. The gods, then, were powers and forces that ruled the world, keeping it in order and harmony and saving it from chaos. Therefore the conception of the divine approached oneness to the extent that the world itself was seen as metaphysically one; this was because the physical world, far from being God's "creation," was a natural emanation or reflection of the divine world. So *Theos* was always, in the final analysis, a predicate of the cosmos.

Together with this essentially pantheistic polytheism, however, the Greek world also had a vague, undefined consciousness of a personal and supra-worldly God. Quite possibly, the concept of Zeus as supreme god often expressed a certain basic monotheism, as did praying to Zeus as a personal "Thou" whose omnipotence is invoked. There are here signs of an openness to "one" who is beyond the world, but an openness that closes up as soon as we claim to be able to say definitely who this "being" we invoke in our misery is. This "god" then changes back into the mystery immersed in the depths of the world: into Law, Justice, the Ideal . . . the divine "that," subject to impenetrable and unquestionable fate.

The religion of the Old Testament was not monotheistic in a metaphysical, static sense, or as the result of a rational religious quest for the ultimate oneness of the world beyond this one. It was the product of Israel's historical experience of Yahweh, the God who intervened through his actions in the world to choose this people and save it. This God imposed himself on the Israelites through his deeds as the only God who had to matter to them, as an absolutely spiritual "person" on whose sovereign freedom not only the history of Israel depended, but also the history of all peoples and the existence of all things, since he was their transcendent creator.

Yahweh is spiritual, absolutely outside the world. This, however, does not mean that his being is diluted in the nebulous abstraction of a metaphysical concept; on the contrary, in his very absolute transcendence of everything earthly, he is always a "he," a specific and unequivocal "Thou," as he sought to show himself in sovereign freedom to his people. This is because Yahweh's historical intervention is not just the distant starting point for his people's knowledge of him: a knowledge that would depend only on a repetitive tradition or progressive development of a "doctrine of God." This intervention is rather the ever-renewed basis of the people's experience of God in the actual history of his liberating action in the world.

Therefore, in undertaking a theological study of God in the Bible, we have to recall the characteristic features of the way this God is revealed in God's historical actions, as the faith of Israel, and then that of the early Christian community, experienced and proclaimed them.[4]

CHAPTER V

The God of the Old Testament

For us Christians, the self-revelation of God that took place in biblical history comes to us through the word of the church: through the preaching of ministers and shared reading in the lay community, listening to one another and together bearing witness among the people. Through this word, God's liberating acts in past history come down to us and enlighten our living faith in present history. This word shows us these acts as forming a whole: the whole of a history whose individual events or situations can be understood only as a "moment" (Greek *kairos*) in an overall process. And the same word shows us this whole dominated by one saving, definitive and central event, qualitatively different from all preceding events: Christ, in his own history and "pasch," in which is proclaimed the definitive entry of the very God of life into the "flesh" of humankind (see DV 1–4).

This means that for Christians there is necessarily a basic identity of experience and conception of God between the Old Testament and the New. We believe that the Christ event brings a definitive and radical communication of God with the world, and therefore we believe that all earlier actions in this biblical history must have an inner orientation toward Christ, that all words accompanying or recalling such actions must prepare for God's definitive word to us in Christ. This is the sense of St

Augustine's teaching—frequently taken up in later theology—that "the New Testament is present hidden in the Old, and the Old Testament is made manifest only in the New."[1] The experience of God in the New Testament is, then, the fullness and manifestation of God's self-revelation that was inchoate and latent in the Old; the Christ event and the word of the New Testament are what give final and unequivocal sense to God's self-revelation in liberating action and prophetic word in the Old. Not everything in the Old Testament mass of deeds and legends, beliefs, words, customs and the like, is equally God's liberating action and self-revelation to God's people; not everything that God chose to teach that people at certain moments in its history is equally valid for us Christians living "in our times" (Heb. 1:2; see Gal. 4:1–11; Matt. 5:17–47; John 1:14–18; Heb. 7:15–19; 8:6–13). Therefore, if we want to know what God wants the Old Testament to signify for us, we have to read it from the historical Jesus Christ and from the word of the New Testament (DV 4).[2]

This basic identity of the "concept" of God in the Old Testament and the New should not, then, be understood as a sort of reduction of what is said in both testaments to a particular metaphysical concept of God. God is not the same in both testaments through having a necessary and unchanging "essence," but through being the same living and supremely free subject, acting in coherent form in both phases of the same history; God is the same in both testaments because the whole of this biblical history, which culminates in the resurrection of Jesus Christ, is the progressive revelation of the free action of the same personal God: action that God has willed to take place in relation to our world, thereby showing us God's "character" as a living "person" who deals with us.[3]

The whole process of historical revelation collected in the Bible consists of events and situations, collective "experiences," theologies and texts, all to be distinguished from one another. The same historical events—forming the faith horizon of the same people—are seen from different angles and with different accents by each generation and socio-religious grouping. The same experiences—at once historical and "spiritual"—are reflected on and projected according to a variety of theological

traditions, which in turn feed and act on one another: those of
the exodus, with their antecedents in the legends of the patriarchs and creation, and their projection through the covenant
into the society in the promised land at the time they were
written; that of David, rooted in Zion and monarchy, and the
messianic hope; that of the Law of holiness, made present in
the Temple and its liturgy; those of the prophets, with their zeal
for justice and hope of a new people; those of wisdom, preoc-
cupied with human behaviour, retribution, and an apocalyptic
projection to God's judgment of the nations. . . . All these are
expressed in literary form through various oral traditions, in
different forms and editions, in documents, books, collec-
tions . . . all more or less juxtaposed, harmonized or synthesized.

We, approaching the Old Testament from the standpoint of
the poor today, can study its theology with a more historical
purpose, method and plan, following the distinct theological and
literary traditions of the Old Testament itself, "situated" in their
time, asking what relevance they have to the situations in which
distinct groups of Christians find themselves today.[4] Alterna-
tively, we can follow a more systematic approach, seeking the
basic constants of the Bible's experience and theology, correlat-
ing them with our own deepest "spiritual experience," and producing a corresponding account of our own Christian faith in
the situation we live in today. Here I propose to follow the
second alternative, with the aim of sketching out a synthesis of
major themes in the experience of the living God that recur as
constants in the Old Testament: a synthesis which can perhaps
help us to find better-founded answers to our problems, and to
broaden the horizon of our journey in faith. Taking this course
inevitably has its limitations: it means skating over the differences and riches that characterize the various theological and
literary traditions, each rooted in the history and distinct social
and religious societies of Israel and pre-Christian Judaism.

Taking the basic constants, the first observation to be made
is that Israel's faith appears dominated by two themes that are
rationally contradictory, but which in reality form the two poles
of this faith as living reality: one is the holiness, the transcendence, the radical difference of God from us and from all reality
that is not God—the "qualitatively infinite distance between

God and ourselves," as Barth put it; the other is that God freely comes to us in love, enters into a direct and complete relationship with us that suppresses all distance.

Other religions also teach that the divinity is great, sublime, and exercises power over us. But here the conception of the divine is rooted in natural powers and phenomena: generation and growth, decay and death. The likeness between the divinity and ourselves and the world is greater than the difference; the divine is really the mystery immanent in the world and life itself. When reason attempts to purify this picture, the sphere of the divine becomes transcendent, divinity itself then becomes infinite, vague, unknowable. Transcendence and closeness are then—as seems logical—in inverse relation to one another: greater transcendence means less closeness, and vice versa.

When we come to the Bible, on the other hand, it is difficult to decide whether to begin with God's holiness or with God's coming close to and communing with us. It is not the case that Israel started with a very elevated conception of the divine transcendence, only later to have its God revealed in saving events and the will to commune. On the contrary, God is revealed to Israel as "the holy one," in an original and unique fashion in comparison with other religions, in the very history and events that save the people and communicate God. One can even say that transcendent holiness is the most outstanding and characteristic feature of the God of the Old Testament, a feature that in a way implies all the others, particularly those of love for and communication with humankind. Transcendence and closeness are here, then—paradoxically—in direct relation to one another: greater closeness means greater transcendence.[5]

This dominant tension or radical paradox needs to be kept in mind as we now deal—in necessarily successive and separate form—with three aspects of the nature and being of God that devolve from God's actions in the history of Israel: the holy God, the God who communes with us, the living God.

1. THE HOLY GOD

(a) *Basic Intuitions*

Isaiah's account of his call (6:1–7) bears witness to an intense experience of the holiness (*kados*) of Yahweh. This holiness is

what makes Yahweh God and not human; it is the radical oth-
erness of God, way beyond the reach of human beings. Bound
up with Yahweh's holiness is his glory (*kabod*): his immensity,
glowing light, exaltation, which can be overwhelming and awe-
inspiring for us. In this sense, God's holiness can be felt as
terrible: our spontaneous reaction to the manifestation of God's
glory is mortal terror, since "no one can see Yahweh and live."
God's holiness then requires that God be separated from us, a
separation shown in liturgy (ritual formulas, church architec-
ture). This is an attempt to safeguard God's holiness from
unwarranted contact with the profane, which would be a *hybris*
(proud daring and sacrilege) on our part, and at the same time,
it is an attempt to safeguard ourselves from the risk of being
harmed by this unpredictable power.

Experience of the "holiness" of the divinity, at once fascinating and terrifying for us mortals, is a factor common to all
religions.[6] This "holiness" is generally perceived as an imper-
sonal power, something poured out over us blindly. In this text
from Isaiah, however, there is a new element: the holy one is
Yahweh, a definite person, who chooses a particular man and
sends him out on a mission and who appears concerned for the
salvation of his people.

In Moses' victory song (Exod. 15), Yahweh's holiness is seen
as the unleashed power of a warrior leader, rising up powerful
and terrible at the head of an exterminating horde. Here too,
however, this terrible character of Yahweh is not seen as the
arbitrary anger of a chaotic force, but as the action of a "someone," of a personal will. It is precisely in this personal character
that Yahweh's holiness appears as an absolute value, independent of us and our desires; and this absolute value is not just the
source of terror and death, but also of salvation and life (see
also 1 Sam. 6:20; Hos. 11:9; Isa. 8:13; 29:23; Ezek. 1:28).

The holiness of Yahweh is seen, then, as fullness of life and
power. This is what the term "Sabaoth" ("of hosts") invokes,
the plural embracing all the powers of heaven and earth. This
is why Yahweh is the source of life, why his works (in history)
are unheard-of, marvellous, and why he shows his holiness in
carrying out these prodigious feats. These wonderful works are
above all interventions to save Israel and punish its enemies. So

the reason for so much emphasis being given to Yahweh's strength as a warrior is not simply to show him as a barbarous and destroying leader, but because this is — in this historical context — the easiest and most convincing way of showing his saving actions as king of Israel (see Isa. 28:21; Num. 20:13; Ezek. 20:24).

Yahweh alone is holy, and he is jealous of his holiness, which he shares with no other. He is jealous of other gods (which centuries later will lead to Israel's monotheism), and — as a result — of other nations (which invoke their own gods). This is why Yahweh continues to intervene on behalf of faithless Israel "for the honour of his name among the nations." So his jealousy is simply the expression of his exclusive holiness, and in turn is passed on to Israel in the shape of the intolerance of the First Commandment: not to adore strange gods. This jealousy, which Hosea expresses in terms of a lover's passion, means that the holiness of Yahweh is that of someone who is a person in the highest grade, of someone who looks on Israel with love, with such a strong love that it cannot tolerate a response from a divided heart.[7] This intolerance becomes a characteristic of the religion of Israel, at a time when cults blended easily into one another, and each left its devotees free to invoke the protection of other gods as well as its own (see Exod. 20:5; 34:14; Deut. 6:14; 18:3; Josh. 24:19; Isa. 9:7; 37:32; 24:8; 59:17; Ezek. 36:22).

Yahweh's jealousy shows as anger when the honour of his name — his love — has been wounded. This anger can be discharged against "the nations" or against Israel itself. This anger, then, is the holiness of God as directed to rebellious human beings. But this anger, like the very holiness it manifests, is incalculable and uncontrollable; it obeys no laws and at times seems to be discharged without reason (see Exod. 4:24; Num. 25:11; Isa. 5:25; Hos. 5:12–14; Jer. 13:12–14; 25:15; Wisd. of Sol. 3:8).

(b) Theological Understanding

(i) Holiness and ritual segregation. Though holiness also extends to particular things, places, times and persons, it always has an intensely personal centre of reference: Yahweh, the only

absolutely holy one, who claims his rights over things and times in order to fill all of human life—not merely the inner life—with his holiness. So the relegation of Yahweh's holiness to a special (ritual) sphere was seen as something transitory. The Priestly Document itself, which gives so much importance to ritual segregation, also looks forward to a time when "the glory of Yahweh fills the earth" (Num. 14:21; see Isa. 6:1–5). "On that day . . . even the ordinary cooking pots of the people . . . will be consecrated to Yahweh" (Zech. 14:20, 21).

(ii) Anger and moral evil. In Israel's tradition, principally as upheld by the prophets, manifestations of Yahweh's anger are increasingly related to human sinfulness and to moral evil. But this is never presented as a law of more or less automatic rewards and punishments stemming from a sort of "immanent justice." On the contrary, the relationship is discovered precisely in understanding sin as directed against the person of Yahweh himself: sin provokes his anger because it wounds his holiness, because it offends the holy love of the God of the covenant. According to the prophets, the worst blasphemy is for us, in our self-sufficiency, to state that God cannot be annoyed by sin (Amos 9:10; Isa. 5:18ff), because such a statement implies the denial of God's holiness. Therefore, too, proclaiming only oracles of peace and prosperity is characteristic of false prophets. As for the origin of human sin, everything that was inspired in human hearts, including evil, was originally attributed to Yahweh. Gradually, however, the instigation of evil came to be attributed to one of the angels or spirits who made up Yahweh's court (see 1 Sam. 16:14ff; 1 Kings 22:22ff). Satan, the tempter angel, later became "the evil one," a doctrine that came from an increasingly ethical and transcendent conception of Yahweh himself, so that evil could not come from him.

(iii) Ritual proscriptions and the ethics of the prophets. The prophets showed Israel that the transgressions that really mattered to Yahweh were not those that broke ritual proscriptions (the primitive idea of violating taboos) but those that offended against love and justice (see Amos 5:21–5; Isa. 1:10–17; 29:13–14; 58:1–12; Mic. 6:6–8; Ps. 50). This brought out, with total clarity, the moral absoluteness of Yahweh's nature: a nature that radically excluded any compromise in matters of truth and jus-

tice. The prophets, feeling themselves to be the mouthpieces of this God, did not spare even the most sacred figures and institutions from their denunciations: the patriarchs (Hosea 12), the Temple worship (Amos, Isaiah, Jeremiah, Deutero-Isaiah), the king (Nathan, Elijah, Hosea, Isaiah, Jeremiah), the priesthood and fortunetelling (the prophets of the eighth and seventh centuries) and so on.

Although holiness cannot be reduced to its ethical dimension, it has to be emphasized that the absolute character of Yahweh's justice is an essential element of his holiness. But his "justice" needs to be examined more closely as conditioned specifically by the covenant, which shows Yahweh's will to enter into communion with us.

2. THE GOD WHO COMMUNES WITH US

For Israel, the intense perception of Yahweh's holiness — breaking all moulds of nature religion — did not weaken but strengthened the experience of Yahweh's communing with human beings: the experience of his "presence" in Israel, of the "knowledge" that pious Israelites had of God (see the Psalms). This was made possible by the strong accent placed on the sovereign freedom of Yahweh in his initiative of communicating himself to human beings. The most prominent features shown in Yahweh's historical communication to Israel are: (a) Yahweh's justice; (b) the God who is faithful in love; (c) the God of the poor.

(a) Yahweh's Justice

"Justice" (*sedaqá*) is not a static feature of the divine "essence," but a dynamic feature of Yahweh's character, shown in his actions. It is the rightness of the actions of Yahweh, who "works" justice. This can have a positive application (when Yahweh "does justice" or "restores justice" in favour of someone) and then coincides with his saving action, or a negative application (when Yahweh "executes justice" against someone). Yahweh's justice clearly shows the dynamic tension between his transcendent holiness and his closeness to humankind: hence the double nature of his justice.

The primary aspect of Yahweh's justice is that it is absolute, sovereign. Yahweh himself, in his holiness, provides the norm for his own actions. All ethical norms are valid as such by their reference to the way Yahweh acts, and he in turn cannot be measured by any humanly conceived norms (see Isa. 1:27; 5:16; 10:22; Wisd. of Sol. 3:5, 8).

Yahweh's justice, however, is also seen as historically conditioned by his own plan of salvation. This applies in the first place to the whole of humankind, seen as a collectivity — see the biblical account of the flood, especially compared to its Babylonian parallels. In the latter the gods decide to destroy the human race, whereas in the biblical account the desire to save it predominates: before carrying out his judgment, Yahweh decides to save Noah, and the human race by means of him; he "judges" not out of anger, but because he "repents" of having created the human race (Gen. 6:5ff). Yahweh's plan of salvation also applies on the individual level: this is seen more clearly as Israel develops concern for individual responsibility and destiny — Yahweh does not want the death of the sinner, but rather that the sinner turn from evil ways and live (Ezek. 18:23).

More specifically, Yahweh's justice is seen as conditioned by the covenant with Israel: it is the loyalty Yahweh shows in the history of his relations with the community formed by the covenant. Although it is linked to the Law as the statute of this community, Yahweh's justice cannot be reduced, here either, to a mere carrying-out of "retributive justice." On the contrary, his justice here — more than ever — appears as a personal quality transcending all laws and frameworks, and assuring continuity of the living relationship that is the final purpose of the Law, offering ever new means of restoring the links broken by human beings. Yahweh's justice, his "judgment," are then seen in his actions taken to restore the covenant, and even to "justify" sinners. This means that this same justice can be invoked as the basis and motive for the forgiveness of sins: in the Psalms, for example, justice and mercy, far from being opposed, are often used in parallel, since both terms express Yahweh's actions in terms of his friendship with us (see 31:2; 33:5; 36:11; 48:10;

85:11; 89:15; 103:17; 143:11; 145:17). Justice is an essentially religious concept, which resists all attempts to water it down in terms of an abstract ethic (see Mic. 7:7–10; Ps. 51:16; Zech. 9:9).

This absolute character of the God of the covenant and his demands for obedience (the Law) gave the Israelites the certainty that Yahweh's actions would follow the same channels of righteousness that he required of them. This too is in contrast to other religions: in the Babylonian cults, for example, despite the importance of oracles and astrology, there was still a terrible uncertainty with regard to the principles on which the divinity could be expected to behave toward human beings; in Israel, on the other hand, the certainty of Yahweh's justice in his dealings with the people appears confirmed by historical examples, in which a particular model of divine dealing can be recognized — this applies especially to the so-called "Deuteronomic history" (Deuteronomy-Kings), in which this model appears most powerfully, though still in an ingenuously schematic form.

The emphasis placed on collective retribution did not obscure the reality of God's will for each member of the community. Even the oldest accounts are full of examples of individuals having direct recourse to Yahweh for the protection of their personal rights. There was an ancient conviction that God finds the suffering of the innocent in place of the guilty intolerable (see Gen. 18:16ff; 2 Sam. 24:10ff). This being said, one can still broadly distinguish two phases in Israel's concept of Yahweh's justice as applied to the people:

1. In the first phase, the *sedaqá* of Yahweh was applied principally to his intervention on Israel's behalf against its external enemies. Yahweh cares for the "justice" of his people in that he safeguards their existence by means of victories over their enemies, and these victories are seen as signs of Yahweh's "judgment." This is why the leaders raised up by Yahweh among the people to be instruments of these "judgments" are known as "judges."

2. Soon, however, greater emphasis came to be placed on the recognition that Yahweh is the protector of rights against all perversions of justice within the people. Just as the Law administered by Moses rested on divine authority, so all laws regulating the conduct of the people derived ultimately from the code

handed down on Sinai. This inner dimension of the justice of
Yahweh was accentuated and deepened by the prophets, who
saw the main threat to the covenant coming, not from outside,
but from within the people themselves. And the content of the
eschatological justice with which Yahweh "will bless" his people
in the new covenant will not be the restoration of Israel's power
among the nations, but the disappearance of all violence and
oppression from within the people, who will then live united by
deep bonds of community, in harmony with Yahweh's plan, his
way of acting in history and his personal character (as foreshad-
owed by the eschatological figure of the "Prince of Peace" in
Isa. 11:1–9 and Ps. 72).

(b) The God Who Is Faithful in Love

Yahweh is the God who has "interfered" in history in order
to take Israel into his service, welcoming it through the covenant
into a relationship of intimacy. The closeness of its God that
Israel experiences as a result does not spring from any "natural"
accessibility, or from any human ability to discern and domesticate the inner motives of divine action. On the contrary, it
stems from an act of sovereign freedom by the "holy one," who
has decided to approach human beings and commit himself to
them in their history. The basis for this communion can be
sought, then, only in the "heart" of God, in the inner source of
God's actions as a person. This is what appears as Moses' intuition in one of the most intense accounts the Old Testament
provides of a human encounter with God (read, successively,
Exod. 24:12–18; 33:18–23; 34:5b–9). It is summed up in the "por-
trait" of Yahweh given in Exodus 34:6: Yahweh is "a God full
of pity [*rahum*] and mercy [*hanún*], slow to anger, and abounding
in constancy [*hesed*] and truth [*hemet*]."

These are images taken from the emotions and attitudes that
most deeply affect our lives as human beings, later applied to
Yahweh with great realism by the prophets: *rahum* is tenderness,
the gut feeling of love and compassion of a mother for her infant;
hanún is the benevolence or favour shown by a ruler (or father)
for his favourite subjects (or children); *hesed* is the love of solidarity and mutual trust of those who are bound by unbreakable

ties of family, friendship or, above all, marriage. These images, especially that of married love, point to the deep seriousness and to the free and gratuitous nature of this love of Yahweh for his people. In the culture of the ancient East, it was exclusively the male's prerogative to choose a wife; so too it was Yahweh's place to take the exclusive initiative to commune with human beings, and he chose and committed his most personal love where there was nothing especially lovable (see Hos. 2:21-2; 11:1-4; Jer. 2:1-3; Isa. 49:14-15).

The faithfulness or "truth" (*hemet*) of Yahweh is another characteristic of his holiness (see Isa. 65:15; Ps. 57:11). Yahweh is the one who stands firm, the sure one, the one in whom one can have confidence (see Isa. 7:9b; 30:15; Jer. 17:5-8). Common images used in this context are of the rock, the only solid base on which to build (Isa. 28:16; Ps. 18:3), or of a mother's arms in which a child can lie in confidence (Ps. 131). More concretely, it is the faithfulness of Yahweh's personal love committed in the covenant: love that is not only constant, but obdurate, remaining steadfast despite the repeated infidelities of his people (see Hos. 2:21-2; Jer. 3:12ff; Isa. 49:15; 54:7-8).[8]

The Old Testament has many examples of pagan peoples being expressly included in God's saving love. But more noticeable are a series of "elections," in which Yahweh appears to distribute his love and hatred arbitrarily among human beings. So he loves Abel, Jacob, the people of Israel, but hates Cain, Esau and the Pharaoh of Egypt. In reflecting on this fact, we need to bear in mind: (1) the personal nature of Yahweh's love; and (2) his plan for universal salvation.

1. The first thing to consider in the accounts of the personal nature of Yahweh's love is the ethical dimension of his "election"; the hated ones also appear to be responsible for an evil, and therefore Yahweh rejects them. Then, "hate" does not necessarily have to be taken in an affective sense: it can often mean "valuing less" (e.g., Deut. 21:15; cf. Luke 14:26 and Matt. 10:37). Finally, and most importantly, "election" is a concrete expression of Yahweh's transcendent holiness and of his love for human beings; his love and forgiveness spring from intensely personal decisions that infinitely transcend human calculations

and do not bow to any human pressure (Exod. 33:18ff; Amos 7).

2. As for the universality which is the final goal of Yahweh's saving plan, the Old Testament has a strongly universalist current running through it, in permanent tension with the particularist or nationalist tendency in Israel's history and religion. So, immediately after the flood, Yahweh comes to make a universal covenant not to destroy humankind again (Gen. 8:12ff [Yahwist]; 9:1–16 [Priestly]); the final purpose of the calling of Abraham is that "in you all peoples of the earth will be blessed" (Gen. 12:1–3); Yahweh is concerned with the Philistines and Nubians as well the Israelites, and his "judgment" threatens Israel as much as its enemies (Amos. 9:7–8); the books of Jonah and Ruth were written to reduce Israelites' particularism in their understanding of their election, and to emphasize that Yahweh's saving purpose extends to all the pagan peoples. Also, Israel's election — like that of all individuals within Israel who receive a special call — is presented as being for a mission or task, aimed at universal salvation. This is most clearly expressed in Deutero-Isaiah: there Yahweh is unequivocally recognized as God of all peoples, who chooses Israel to take his covenant to the nations (Isa. 45:20–25; 42:1–9; 49:1–6).

(c) The God of the Poor

All that has been said about Yahweh's justice among the people and his compassionate love applies in a special way to the poor, the outcasts and the oppressed generated by the social and economic history of Israel.

(i) The God who freed Israel from Egypt. For Israel, Yahweh is the God who heard the cry of his poor in Egypt (Exod. 3:7–10) and who appeared to them by freeing them through the exodus and then during the time of their settlement in the promised land. Throughout the whole of their history, the people of Israel recall that when their fathers were oppressed and reduced to slavery and poverty, God was good to them and they were able to celebrate the first Passover. Once settled in Palestine, the people of Israel regard this as a revelation of the nature of their God, which in turn commits them in their dealings with

the poor in their midst: "If your brother becomes poor and is unable to support himself, help him that he may continue to live with you, at least as a stranger and a guest. Do not take interest from him. . . . I am Yahweh, your God, who brought you out of the land of Egypt to give you the land of the Canaanites and to be your God" (Lev. 25:35–38). And so too, with greater reason: "You shall not wrong or oppress a stranger, for you were strangers in the land of Egypt. You shall not harm the widow or the orphan. If you do harm them and they cry out to me, I will hear them . . . for I am full of pity" (Exod. 22:20–26). The theme of the "cry" of the oppressed and Yahweh as the one who "hears" that cry runs through the whole Bible: the historical traditions, the preaching of the prophets and, above all, the prayers of the Psalms.

(ii) Yahweh's kingly justice. During the period of the monarchy, the God of the poor is revealed above all when social injustices and breaches of the covenant abound, to the detriment of the humble and downtrodden. The prophets then raise their protest against all injustice: against the insolent luxury and insatiable greed of the upper classes, who trample on the poor and the needy (Amos 5:7–27; Isa. 1:10–20; Mic. 6:5–8; Zech. 7:4–14). The God of the covenant is then presented as implanting his saving justice by restoring the rights of the downtrodden. Underlying this conviction is the idea of the justice of Yahweh as king of Israel (see Pss. 76:8–10; 147:7–10; 10:16–18). In effect, the peoples of the ancient Middle East expected their kings to act as protectors of the poor, orphans and widows, the weak and oppressed; their duty was seen to be that of assuring justice to all their subjects—which meant in practice to those who were incapable of standing up to the powerful and their oppressors on their own. So Yahweh too, as king of Israel characterized by kingly justice, was the protector of the weak and the poor.

This was not done through some form of retributive justice, rewarding supposed merits acquired by the poor through their piety and trust in God ("spiritual" poverty): it was a sort of "regal" justice, in which it behoved God to guarantee the rights of the downtrodden. The full effects of this divine justice were still not in evidence, but were to appear one "day" when Yahweh would fully establish his Reign on earth. Then—as the pro-

phetic oracles insist in the darkest days of the people's history—
the afflicted and the hungry will be avenged on all who oppress
them and will be able to enjoy the divine "blessing" to the full.
And this "blessing," throughout the Bible, is usually specified
as an abundance of goods enjoyed in happy thankfulness with a
cordial gathering of companions and friends, an enjoyment seen
as a sacrament of communion with the God of life (see Jer.
31:7–14; Isa. 29:18–119; 35:3–6; 49:9–13; Ezek. 24:11–29). The
God who "has put down the mighty from their thrones and lifted
up those who are downtrodden," who "has filled the hungry with
good things but has sent the rich away empty" (Luke 1:52–3), is
thus seen as the embodiment of the ideal king, from a viewpoint
that does not idealize poverty, but presents a theology of God's
justice and the hope of the Kingdom to come.

This God of the poor commits those faithful to the covenant
to serve their fellows suffering poverty and oppression. This is,
conclusively, what makes a person agreeable in the eyes of God:
"To break the fetters of injustice and unfasten the thongs of the
yoke, to set the oppressed free and break every yoke. Fast by
sharing your food with the hungry, bring to your house the
unsheltered needy, clothe those you see naked and do not turn
away from your own kin" (Isa. 58:6–7; see also Job 29:12–17;
Ecclus. 4:1–6, 8–10).

(iii) The Messiah of the poor. Pointing to the same aspect of
kingly justice, the eschatological figure of the messianic king, the
vicar of Yahweh, is described with the features of a Davidic
prince who will "defend the cause of the poor, deliver the children of the needy, and crush the oppressor. . . . He delivers the
needy who call on him, the afflicted with no one to help them"
(Ps. 72:4, 12; see Isa. 9:4–5). For this purpose he will be anointed
with the spirit of Yahweh: "to bring good news to the poor. He
has sent me to bind up broken hearts, to proclaim liberty to the
captives, freedom to those languishing in prison . . ., to give com-
fort to all who grieve . . . and give them a garland instead of
ashes, oil of gladness instead of mourning, and a garment of
praise instead of despair" (Isa. 61:1–3; see 11:1ff). Here the
Messiah appears with features of a prophet; so does the "Servant" of Deutero-Isaiah, who comes humbly and peacefully to
be an instrument of salvation to the downtrodden people, taking

upon himself the weight of their suffering and sin (Isa. 42:1–9; 49:1–6; 50:4–9; 52:13–53:12; see Zech. 9:9–10).[9]

3. THE LIVING GOD

The Old Testament puts forward no systematic concept of God: it has no religious philosophy or dogmatic theology; it contains no fixed image of God, in either plastic or conceptual terms; nor does it accept unconditionally a fixed dwelling place for God (see 2 Sam. 7, with the JB's note to v. 13). This, clearly, is because God is holy and therefore transcends all human imagery; it is also because God is the living God (*'el hay*), in permanent and dynamic activity, who cannot be grasped in a static conception, since his revelation is never concluded. The Old Testament speaks of the actions of Yahweh, diverse and paradoxical, in the most divergent situations and forms, in nature and above all in history, but only in the symbolic and concrete language of religious faith.

The decisive feature of this living, essentially dynamic force is its intensely and explicitly personal nature. This, as we have seen, appears first in the sovereign freedom with which Yahweh intervenes in history. This is how Israel knows that its God is the holy one, jealous of his holiness: it has experienced his justice, which transcends every mould, and his gratuitous love, which has no basis other than his will.[10] This decisive feature also appears in two other important elements in Old Testament language about God: the use of the name of God, and the conception of God in human imagery.

(a) The Name of God

(i) *The fact that God has a name.* In effect, the intensely personal manner in which God appears in his actions is shown by, amongst other things, the close link between his interventions and a "name" of God. It is God's own self-revelation that gives this name, showing that people have to refer to him and interpret him as "someone" distinct and individual. In so doing, the faith of Israel declares itself unmistakably against an intellectual and abstract concept of a "supreme being" outside human history, and also against any vague mystical sense of a "vital medium" or "basis of existence." The God of Israel is "someone" who intervenes in the freedom of his love in human life and history, "someone" who can be called by name.

Furthermore, in ancient Eastern culture, a "name" was not just the phonetic sign that served to identify an individual by distinguishing him or her from all others. There was also a close link between the name and the very being and identity of the person the name designated, so that knowing someone's name in a sense gave access to the innermost depths of that person. The "name" of God, then, meant for the Israelites not only a practical means of designating God, from outside, as it were, but also the living sign of God's personal intimacy, the secret of which God had chosen to reveal to those he had chosen as his friends – a living sign that gave them the possibility of recourse to his intervention, that opened up access to his very being. So using God's "name" implied for Israel the conviction that God "answers" when someone (or the people) called on him in specific circumstances in their history, when in moments of anguish they "called on his name."

Such a conception, of course, brings the danger of using the name of God as magic, claiming to use his power to suit one's own needs. This danger is recognized in the Old Testament, but there seem to be two elements that insure the transcendence of the person called on by "the name": the fact that the God of Israel has no need (as other gods have) to keep his name secret, but can communicate it for free use by his faithful without compromising his sovereign freedom, and the fact that he threatens serious consequences for all who take his name "in vain" (Second Commandment), thereby educating people to take God seriously as a person and not as some thing or force that can be "utilized." These elements insured that Israel did not in fact come to abuse the name of its God through magic. The certainty that the divine "name" constituted a guarantee of God's saving presence was always recognized as a sovereign grace coming from God alone: from a God who is beyond the reach of any human pressure, and who preserves his freedom vis-à-vis the faithful who call on him.

(ii) The meaning of the names of God. Besides the general fact

that God has a personal name in the Old Testament, there is the specific meaning of the different names under which God appears. All these names—from El and its derivatives on—underline the personal character of the God named. They designate God not through his natural ties with cosmic phenomena, but through his historical links with individuals or groups of people, frequently alluding to the personal dealings God has had with them (see the account of the religion of the patriarchs in section 2a of the introduction to this part). This is particularly true of the "name" under which God appears above all in the Old Testament: that of Yahweh. In the Exodus text where the revelation of this name to Moses is recounted (Exod. 3:13ff), its significance appears in connection with the verb "to be" (*hayah,* possibly through the archaic Canaan form *hawah*). In the context, the fact that God should "be" does not have an abstract, ontological sense, but the concrete sense of "being for someone," of "being present" (see Hos. 1:9): the sense of being next to someone in an attitude of active solidarity, of attentive willingness to help.

This same conviction is expressed constantly in the Old Testament in the recognition that Yahweh marches at the head of Israel, that his "presence" dwells in their midst, or—simply—that Yahweh, as God of Israel, is a living God. For Yahweh to be a living God means specifically that he is always awake, alert, with a personal and watchful interest in his people (see Ps. 18:47; Hos. 2:1). Hence the formula with which God is invoked as witness to an oath: "The Lord lives" (*hay yahweh*). Hence too the fact that the great scepticism or incredulity that the prophets denounce in the people is not about the "existence" of God, but rather has to do with doubting that Yahweh sees or hears what those who oppress their fellows are doing (see Isa. 29:15; Ps. 10:4, 11).

Yahweh is, in effect, a God who places himself alongside human beings, closely concerned with their lives and behaviour, and who makes the demands of his will felt in their actual history. This will demands submission not in the colourless and general way of an abstract ethic, nor in the blind and fateful manner of a "historic destiny," but as that of a living person committed to a particular human community, in the details of its present life as well as in the broad sweep of its collective history. Such a will cannot then be conceived as a dark and unconscious life force; it can, on the contrary, be conceived only by analogy with human beings: as "someone" who knows, feels, loves, makes a commitment and requires a response.[11]

(b) God in the Image of Human Beings

The more this specific image of God as a person is stressed, the greater the danger of bringing God too close to humankind, thereby threatening God's transcendence. This is particularly obvious in the Old Testament's frequent use of strongly anthropomorphic expressions (attributing parts of the human body, physical actions, local movement and so on to God), or anthropophatic ones (attributing human feelings and emotions to God, such as becoming angry, feeling compassion, repenting, rejoicing, etc.).

Such usage can be explained in part as belonging to the literary genre employed, which is often highly poetical or simply ingenuous. But this explanation does not quite cover the fact that, particularly in the primitive period, God was conceived not only in terms of human personality, but also as though he literally had a physical mode of life and of self-revelation. The accounts given in the Yahwist Document bring this out especially strongly: God comes to Abraham in human form and converses with him, and Yahweh meets Moses face to face in a certain place. This is even more true when these accounts tell of prehistoric times: Yahweh walks in the garden of Eden, comes to talk to Cain, closes the door of Noah's ark from outside, comes down to see what is going on when the Tower of Babel is being built. . . . This sort of expression, however, needs to be kept in its religious context, and it does not prevent an author like the "Yahwist" from having an extremely exalted concept of Yahweh as God of the whole world; nor does it damage the deeply spiritual and ethical character of his accounts. On the broader biblical front, the religious leaders of Israel did not seem to consider these physical aspects of the conception of God to be particularly dangerous. Even the major prophets make abundant use of strongly anthropomorphic and anthropophatic expressions (see, e.g., Isa. 30:27; Hos. 5:14). This produced problems for the formalist Judaic mentality of the last centuries before Christ, especially in its contact with the allegorical interpretation of the school of Alexandria. The prophets clearly thought it important that the people should know about the immaterial nature of Yahweh, but they also thought it important that the people keep a lively grasp of the intensely personal quality of Yahweh's actions and demands.

Religious history provides an explanation for this: it can be shown that whenever a dogmatically based concept of the spirituality of God appears, the immediacy of religious life is dimmed and effective communion with God weakened. As preoccupation with conceptual purity becomes dominant, so religion is diluted, either into a cold deism or an abstract ethic, or into pantheistic speculations; religious experience is then sought in a mysticism of the emotions, or in exotic phenomena produced by esoteric groups. This is why the Christian faith alone can combine a living expression of recognition of the spiritual nature of God with immediacy of practice: its centre is in the historical person of Jesus as unequivocal "sacrament" of the personality of God and of the fully human nature of God's communion with us.[12]

(c) Personality and Transcendence

(i) Yahweh's life transcends human limitations. The religion of Israel, while emphasizing—through its conceiving of God in human imagery—experience of Yahweh as a living person in direct and concrete touch with human beings, at the same time guarded against any tendency to submit God excessively to human limitations. All encounters with God in the Old Testament are dominated by an intense feeling of the immense superiority of the divine being over all merely human attributes and capabilities. This is found even in the primitive accounts of God's familiar dealings with the patriarchs: there is nothing in these to compare with the egalitarian "companionship" between gods and human beings found not only in the Greek myths, but also in many of the Egyptian, Babylonian and Indian ones as well.

Perception of God as a living person can be expressed only through human imagery, but in Israel this perception also implies that God is above all physical needs. Yahweh, as "living God," not only lives, but by definition possesses an inexhaustible life, which is the source of all life (see Jer. 2:13; 17:13; Deut. 30:20; Ps. 36:10). Furthermore, Yahweh proves his vitality, the reality of his existence as living God, through his unceasing and inexhaustible activity — in contrast to the gods of the pagans, who are inert, empty, non-existent (see Jer. 10:1–16; Isa. 40–43; Ps. 135:5ff).

As Israel reflected on this supreme life that characterizes Yahweh, so it began specifically to exclude the limitations that circumscribe human life and personality from it. An example of this can be found in as old a text as the Elijah cycle, where the prophet's mocking of Baal (1 Kings 18:26–29) implies that Yahweh alone is unlimited fullness of life. The same implication was later expressed in doctrinal axioms: God does not sleep (Ps. 121:4); he has no need of eyes, as we have (Job 10:4); "Yahweh does not judge as man judges; man sees the appearance; Yahweh sees the heart" (1 Sam. 16:7; see Pss. 44:22; 139:23); Yahweh does not lie or repent, as human beings do (Num. 23:19); his reactions and feelings are not like human ones (Hos. 11:7–9).

(ii) Yahweh as spirit, God of life. In the prophetic writings, the contrast between the fragile, passing earthly life and the powerful, inexhaustible life of God is usually stressed through the double opposition found in Isaiah 31:3: *adam* (humankind) / *El* (God); *basar* (flesh) / *ruah* (spirit). Neither of these two pairs of terms sets out to mean that God is "spirit" as opposed to "matter" (the principle of physical reality). "Spirit" is rather the very life of God, perceived as inexhaustible energy and power, source of all life; "flesh" is earthly life, essentially weak, transitory and lacking its own vital principle. For the faith of Israel, in effect, wherever there is life, this is Yahweh's gift: he, and he alone, provides the benefits of nature (see Hos. 2; Jer. 31:10–14; Ps. 104). So living with Yahweh means prosperity and abundance of goods for Israel (see Deut. 7:9–15; 8:7–10; 28:1–14). The God of Israel is not "spiritual" in an abstract sense, as if relating to him involved only the inner life of an individual; on the contrary, Israel sees its God wherever there is abundance, salvation and

joy shared among friends. The spiritual and physical spheres are not opposed, still less mutually exclusive, in Hebraic thought. So the major prophets, even with their intense perception of the transcendent vitality of God, continue to speak of God not only in physical images, but also in terms that embrace all dimensions of human life.

CHAPTER VI

The God of Jesus
of Nazareth

1. OUR JOURNEY IN FAITH

The renewed experience of a God who has acted and still acts in the history of the poor has been strongly marked by the rediscovery of Jesus the man, who lived and committed himself in a public ministry and a definite history. Church-educated pastoral agents have contributed to this rediscovery, bringing something of the route followed by European and North American biblical studies and theology, but the form it takes among our oppressed and believing people is a long way from pondering the choice posed since the early years of this century in Europe between the "Jesus of history" and the "Christ of faith."

The concern in the world of the poor, what gives us new birth and sets us free, is the rediscovery of the full humanity of Jesus Christ, Son of the Father and risen Lord, with whom we live today in the communion of faith; the rediscovery of that public and fully historical life that Jesus lived at one time, among one people and in a well-defined set of social and cultural conditions. We rediscover the historical Jesus in and from the communion we have now with Christ in those two inseparable "settings" for our Christian faith: the people of the poor, with the beliefs and practices of their popular Catholicism and liberating solidarity, and the ecclesial community made up of these same poor, with

their physical fellowship, their proclamation and celebration of
the word, their service to one another. It is here, against this
backdrop of faith and in this concern for practical following of
Jesus in our present historical conditions, that we feel the
renewed need to call to mind the journey Jesus once took: the
attitudes he took and choices he made in his circumstances, the
welcome or resistance he aroused in the persons and social
groups with whom he came in contact, the crises and the drama
he lived out to the end. In other words, we today feel the need
to read Jesus' story in the Gospels in the same believing spirit
and with the same type of practical concerns as inspired the
early church to write these Gospels.[1]

In Latin America ordinary people are devoting themselves to
reading the Gospels; this is new in Latin American Catholicism,
and it is purifying and enriching our Christian faith by deepening
and renewing its reference to a concrete Jesus. This Jesus of the
Gospels, who showed us the Father's love, plan and call, lived
in a particular historical setting that has many deep similarities
to our own. He showed the Father's love through human actions
and gestures, through concrete historical decisions and liberating practices, which are the inescapable measure of Christian
life and duty, and of the communal and ministerial life of the
church. These are, and should always have been, the indispensable reference point of our Christian faith and of our actual
journey in faith. This is the only way we can prevent the "Christ
of our faith" and our very image of God being vapourized as
more or less unconscious projections of our longings and nos-
talgias, or converted into idols as a sacred legitimation of our
own personal or group habits and interests.

As was said earlier (at the end of chapter I), this rediscovery
of the historical Jesus in our belief and commitment is more
and more colouring our very experience of God. In this way,
almost without noticing it, we are moving farther from the structure of the catechesis we learned, insofar as this often consisted
in a simplified summary of the "scholastic" content of seminary
theology. This started with the existence of God, "explained" in
the language of philosophical speculation; went on with the
Trinity, as a "secret" revealed to Christians; went on to explain
Jesus as one of the persons of this Trinity—the Son—who came

to earth, was incarnated, founded the church and then went
back to the Father. This structure seemed to suppose that God's
existence was a more or less self-evident reality to us, and that
the "mystery" of the Trinity was a sort of enigma designed to
remind us of God's transcendence.

In real life, however, we cannot definitely know the true God,
nor can the Trinity have any meaning for us, without encoun-
tering this singular person called Jesus of Nazareth. This means
that without this encounter with the historical Jesus, the God
we evoked in our theology was often more like the supreme
principle known through the philosophical speculation of intellectual elites than the Father revealed to little ones, more like
the almighty invoked by ruling-class ideology than the liberator
of the oppressed and avenger of the downtrodden. And in the
same way we projected an image of Christ as a heavenly per-
sonage, often confused with this mythical figure of an all-pow-
erful and distant God.

Now, on the other hand, we approach things the other way
round, as it were. In the foreground we place Jesus of Nazareth,
the historical figure whose messianic story is told in the Gospels.
It is Jesus, the Christ, who testifies to the Kingdom of God as
an active dynamism of liberation among the poor, who personally lives and brings us back into communion with the Father
and with our brothers and sisters, who is rejected by those who
feel safe and hold power, sentenced by the authorities and put
to death on the cross. God, then, appears in indirect form: God
as such is not the prime or central theme in Jesus' teaching, nor
the direct "object" of Christian experience. What we actually
experience and practise, what we suffer and make, is our own
human history. But in this human history of liberating solidarity—that of Jesus and our own "in his name"—the living God
becomes immediately present with God's liberating love. This is
the God of the Kingdom, the Father of Jesus Christ, who raised
Christ crucified from among the dead, who gives us the Spirit
of the risen Lord so that we too can take up his cause and follow
the same path, and thereby "do" truth and "know" God (see
John 3:21; 1 John 3:16–24; 4:7–12; Eph. 4:15).

Through our catechesis and theology, we seek to deepen our
knowledge of the specific dynamic of following Jesus and to

reflect on the basis and content of faith in our meeting with Jesus Christ. The Gospel story shows that the way to understand following Jesus is through journeying with the oppressed people seeking their liberation. The God whom we evoke and invoke in this way is the liberator God, living and true, the God we experience through following Jesus and carrying out his liberating practice in the history of our people.

As Christians, we know that Jesus is not just the latest of the prophets of Israel, the foremost witness to God produced by our history and tradition, not just the greatest religious genius and teacher of truth known to humankind. . . . As Christians, we believe precisely that this actual person—Jesus of Nazareth—is, for the whole world and the whole of history, the Christ of God, the only Son equal to the Father, the Word through which God has spoken to and definitively communicated with the world of human beings. We believe and proclaim that this particular individual—who lived in specific historical circumstances and there risked his life for the liberation of humankind—is the full and final revelation of the one living and true God (see DV 1–4).[2]

This is why early Christian preaching and the whole of the New Testament lay such stress on the call to "follow Jesus," to "believe in the Son," to "accept the Word" and.respond to it with one's whole life; why they insist that "only [he has] the words of eternal life," that he alone—in his actual history and practice—is "the way, the truth and the life." And this is why early Christian theology and the creeds attributed such decisive importance to affirming the full divinity of Jesus and his equality to the Father: because this very Jesus and he alone—Mary's son, crucified under Pontius Pilate, as human and historical as we—is the "only Son of God, born of the Father before all ages, God [proceeding] from God, light from light, true God from true God . . ., of one being with the Father" (DS 150).

So it is the witness Jesus bore to God through his life that, for us Christians, forms the ultimate criterion for judging all religious faith, any experience or concept of God, both among us today and in the texts of the biblical tradition itself. This applies (as we saw in part 2) to images and perceptions of God current in our society today, and (as we saw in the preceding chapter) to the different dimensions of God shown in the biblical tradition itself, with its long and complex evolution tied to the vicissitudes and history of a very earthly people. Therefore, it is natural for us to be left with an impression of uncertainty, of a certain relativism, a sense that we all believe in God in our own way, that one can find a bit of everything in the Bible.... This is so, and always has been, to a large extent. The history of biblical exegesis and Christian confessions of faith, not to mention an even superficial analysis of the divergent tendencies within contemporary Christianity, are ample illustration of this.

In fact, however, if we are honest with ourselves, we have to say that this relativism is restricted if we take the gospel of Jesus Christ seriously. In the conflictive and religiously ambiguous time and culture in which Jesus lived, he made definite choices, acting against many of the ruling religious and social practices, committed himself to correcting misunderstandings and deformations of the concept of God revealed by these practices, and, finally, was condemned and executed for his consistent witness to a God who contradicted the "God" of the socio-political and religious establishment. This witness Jesus gave, confirmed by God who raised him from among the dead, has given us the definitive key for recognizing the true face of the living God, distinguishing it from caricatures and falsifications, in any age and any social or ecclesiastical setting. (The facility to make this radical distinction does not, of course, remove all problems, since Jesus' testimony does not come to us direct, but mediated through the texts of the Gospels and the living tradition of the church, both of which we have to read and interpret anew in our own situation. This is why I have already pointed out the need to discover the "viewpoint" and the "hermeneutical principles" needed to make our reading faithful and pertinent.)

2. HOW JESUS REVEALS GOD TO US

We now need to take a closer look at how Jesus gives this witness to God. I propose to make eight points:

1. Jesus' witness to God is a particular and specific one. In view of the foregoing, this may seem obvious, but it is basic, and needs to be developed a little further.

We cannot tell in advance, from what we already knew of
God, what this witness "had to be": what we need is information
on or "notice" of where and how it was, as a matter of historical
fact. The fact is that Jesus' witness was contingent or "situated":
not just in space and time, but within an actual society, with its
contrasts and conflicts, and in a particular cultural and religious
setting, also complex and shot through with tensions. Jesus bore
his witness from a very definite "social setting," in certain conditions and in a particular language. If the technical means had
existed, we could have had a visual record of Jesus, not to say
a recording of his words, a documentary record of the events in
which he was involved. This might not have made his witness
any more accessible: we might be put off by his unkempt appearance, his "bad taste," might suspect him of populism, be irritated
by his radicalism, find his direct manner of speaking ill-man-
nered, his whole approach aggressive. If he appeared among us
and behaved in exactly the same way, we should almost certainly
be disappointed at not getting the sort of answers we expected.
He would scandalize us—as he did so many of his contempo-
raries—by not confining his mission to the areas we had sub-
consciously assigned to him, by spoiling our certainties, by
making impossible demands on us. . . . As believers, we know
that this same Jesus is the holy one of God, the Son. But we
can know who this Christ of faith is for us, and "know" the God
of this holy one, the Father, only by taking this particular person
seriously: by understanding his language, his manner of being,
the choices he made, as told to us in the story of his particular
history found in the Gospels. If we stray from this path, we are
exposed to the whims and ambiguities of our religious feelings,
of our ideology or speculations; we are open to the old Gnostic
tendency to conceive of a very celestial Christ, a God far above
everything material and earthly . . . but imaginary.

2. Jesus' witness to God is found not just in what he said, but
above all in what he did: his actions, his choices, and the particular messianic strategy they reveal. John the Baptist's question: "Are you the one we are expecting . . . ?" was answered not
with verbal explanations, but simply with: "Go back and tell
John what you saw and heard: the blind see again, the lame
walk, lepers are made clean, the deaf hear, the dead are raised

to life, and the poor are given good news" (Luke 7:18–22). Of
course his teaching and discourse are important and essential
too. And the words just quoted, besides referring to his actions,
also implicitly situate them in the framework of the hope kept
alive in the people through the prophetic tradition (see Isa.
26:19; 35:5–6; 61:1). But his words are always a component part
of Jesus' messianic activities, together with his deeds, his
increasingly defined strategy and his particular approach.

3. So Jesus' witness is not to be found in discourse isolated
from his practice, nor in practice separated from the actual situation of the bulk of the people. It is found rather in the particular relationship between his practice, his surroundings and
his discourse. Jesus' practice, the coherence of his actions,
stands in relationship to the real lives of the people around him,
to the social and religious—not to mention economic, political,
cultural and ideological—situation of his people and that society. Jesus' words, his discourse and teaching, explain the meaning of that practice, and like it refer to the actual situations of
people: they judge those situations, pronounce on history and
decipher it in the light of the biblical tradition. So we today
need to know those situations and that particular history of
Jesus' people and time, if we are to discover the more precise
meaning of his practice and the message that goes with it.

4. By the same token, Jesus' words about God are not direct,
let alone systematic, teaching. He does not speak about God in
the way a professor of theology, or a catechist assigned the "subject," might. In any case, the main "subject" of Jesus' preaching
is not so much the nature of God as the coming of God's Kingdom—at that "moment"—to this earth of ours. And Jesus' very
discourse on this Reign of God's—and therefore on the God
who is coming to reign—is indirect, paradoxical, and open. We
cannot find a direct, logically articulated, self-enclosed doctrine
in his words. These words rather spring up along his way according to circumstances, accompany and explain his actions, allude
to specific situations, reply to questions . . ., and do so through
images or stories, allusions, parrying a question with another;
they disconcert, involve and question his audience, suggest
unexpected horizons of freedom and life, invite committed
search. . . .

5. Jesus' witness to God is conflictive and polemical, running counter to the dominant religious practices and concepts of his world. We can sometimes imagine that the religion of the Jewish people at the time of Jesus was exactly the faith of the Old Testament. But this is not the case—and of course, the Old Testament is full of different currents and layers. In the Palestine of Jesus' time, the religious situation was complex and even confused: there was the religious theology and ideology of the Temple priests, tied to the interests of the wealthy and conciliatory toward the Roman occupation; there was the religious leadership of the Pharisees, with their casuistical interpretation of the Law and their nationalism; there were the various currents of popular messianism and apocalyptic hope, often extreme. . . . In this milieu, Jesus' witness breaks established patterns, disconcerts, provokes resistance—as shown in the arguments with religious leaders that fill so many pages of our Gospels. And much of his positive teaching—in the parables, for example—comes across as justification of his actions. His often disconcerted listeners are shown the way God acts and the personal nature of God, revealed in Jesus' own actions as popular prophet and Messiah of the poor.

Jesus legitimates his behaviour by explaining that this is how God acts, that God is actually like this, not like what the priests, teachers of the Law and Pharisees would have people believe (see, e.g., Luke 10:1–37; 14:1–24; 15:1–32). But Jesus' witness is also more overtly polemical in that it unmasks the falsifications of God implicit in the dominant religion. And so his harshest words are found in John, the evangelist of God's love: "Why do you not understand my teaching? It is because . . . the father you spring from is the devil and you will carry out the evil wishes of your father, who has been a murderer from the beginning. . . . He is a liar, and the father of lies" (John 8:43–44). The priests and teachers claim that they know God, whereas in reality their religion is lying and murderous idolatry, service of the devil (see John 5:7–10).

6. The witness to God that Jesus bore throughout his public life achieves its full meaning for us only in the light of his final destiny. That is, the cross and the resurrection cannot be separated from one another. Jesus' arrest and sentencing to death

can be explained only as the outcome of his conflict with the
authorities, together with the fact that his actions and manner
were more and more out of keeping with many of the expectations of popular messianism. In turn, Jesus' trial, violent death
and—more radically—the absolutely astonishing event of his
pasch shed light retrospectively on his life and practice among
the people. (The four Gospels we have are in fact re-readings
of the memory of Jesus in the light of these final events.)

Jesus' quarrels with the authorities and his suffering at their
hands had a strong social and political connotation, but the more
basic conflict was a religious one. Not only did Jesus act as a
Messiah different from what people expected, his messianic
actions also bore witness to a God different from what people
conceived. In the end it was because of this, nothing less, that
he was abandoned by the crowd and sentenced by the authorities. And in the final analysis it was this, nothing less, that was
confirmed and definitively revealed when his God raised up the
crucified Jesus. From this supreme "moment" on, the living God
is not only the one who, under the old covenant, "freed our
fathers" from slavery in Egypt, but the one who—more radically—"raised Jesus Christ" from among the dead: the God who
made this "stone rejected by the builders" the foundation-stone
of the new covenant, the firstborn of a multitude of brothers
and sisters, head and life-principle of a new humanity and a new
creation (see Acts 2:22–36; 3:13–18; 4:10–11; 1 Pet. 2:4–10; Eph.
1:9–10, 20–23; Col. 1:15–20).

7. If Jesus' witness to God attains its full meaning only with
the cross and resurrection, this means that we can grasp this full
meaning only from the witness of those who experienced the
risen Christ. The only valid viewpoint on this full meaning is
that of those who met the risen Christ, who "ate and drank with
him," knowing him for the same person as had shared their
"comings and goings" till his arrest and sentence. In other
words—applying the witness of Jesus' companions to present
circumstances—we can "know" the God who raised the crucified
Jesus only in the believing community, the community brought
together by the double witness of apostolic preaching and the
Spirit of the same risen Christ. In the final analysis, it is this
Spirit of the Son—made manifest through inspiring mutual love

and enriching the community with its gifts and charisms — that bears witness in us and makes us, in all truth, cry out "Our Father. . . ."

8. So, we today experience the discovery and proclamation of the God of Jesus Christ in a process that can be summed up as the mutual relationship between the word of the Gospels, the believing community and our historical situation. The word brings us the memory of Jesus, of what he did and said in his own situation, in the light of the paschal experience; the community today reads this word in the experience of the solidarity of the Kingdom, thereby prolonging Jesus' messianic activity in the midst of the people; our historical situation is viewed from the standpoint of the poor and oppressed, leading us to commit ourselves to their cause in actual liberating actions. The word of the Gospel feeds the faith of the community and sheds light on collective history; the believing community, in communion with the church and in its historical commitment, (re-)reads this word and with it sheds light on its practice of solidarity.

3. THE GOD OF THE KINGDOM

Now that the church has been "relocated" in the world and among the poor majorities, we are rediscovering the universality of Jesus' mission and witness as concrete universality. This means that it is not a universality viewed (supposedly) "from heaven," or "from a neutral centre," but more consciously from a particular historical situation, from a definite cultural "world," from a specific social setting. We are rediscovering the uniqueness of Jesus' life, the partiality of his choices and message, the fully historical and "situated" nature of his incarnation. We are rediscovering that the Word of God, God's only Son, became incarnate not only "among us," but in a culture and people marginal to the world of his time, and, within this people, in a sector of society that was oppressed by the rest of society and the religious authorities.

As we learn to live with the oppressed people and to allow the griefs and hopes of the poor to flood into our church community and prayer, we are rediscovering together with the poor just how far Jesus' actions and message point to integral human liberation, to the radical changing of all dimensions of human life and society, starting from our most basic needs and rights. This experience has taught us to overcome the distinction we used to make between faith and life, between the history of God's salvation and the history of human liberations, between love of God and love of one's neighbour, between the task of evangelization and that of human advancement and liberation, between historical hopes and the hope of ultimate fullness of life and our coming together with God in the final encounter.

On these twin tracks, of concrete universality and integral human liberation, the rediscovery of the gospel theme of the Kingdom or Reign of God has played a decisive role. In reality, this is not just one "theme," but the living reality that forms the nucleus of Jesus' preaching and the raison d'être of the whole of his historic ministry. We are rediscovering that God's Reign — as Jesus proclaimed it and showed it already present through his historical stance and concrete gestures — comes to us from below, through the "hidden door" of the oppressed and marginalized; comes from there with "signs" and "powers" that heal bodily and spiritual wounds, liberate the oppressed, prepare for and anticipate the fullness of life and communion, . . . in the encounter with the God of life, the universal Father.

Jesus' witness to the God of the Kingdom is borne historically, in deeds and words, alluding to God indirectly and paradoxically, by contrast to the dominant religious images and practices. So the specific content of this witness needs to be sought in the great confrontations in practice and polemic constantly recurring in the Gospel narratives: confrontations between the God of Jesus Christ and the deformations or falsifications of God dominant in his society. These can be divided into four groups: (a) the God of the beatitudes, opposed to the god of the rich and satisfied; (b) the God of the Kingdom, opposed to the god of the powerful; (c) the God of the Suffering Servant, opposed to the god of the popular messianism of the Zealots; (d) the God of mercy and life, opposed to the god of the scribes and Pharisees, of the Temple. These four types of confrontation do not, of course, simply run parallel to one another, but overlap and converge. They are four viewpoints, conditioned by distinct groups or tendencies in his historical setting, from which to form

a more definite understanding of the one living and true God
to whom Jesus of Nazareth bore witness. Let us now take each
of these confrontations in two steps: (i) a reading guide to the
principal passages of the Gospels in which they appear, with
reference to other passages; and (ii) a brief summary of each
confrontation between the God of Jesus and the opposing god.

(a) The God of the Beatitudes, Opposed to the God of the Rich and Satisfied

(i) Reading Guide

Theme: The poor and those who are hungry are blessed, and
the Kingdom is coming to them. The rich, those who oppress
the poor, who feast in the sight of the hungry, are condemned.
Readings: Luke 1:46–55; 6:20–26; 14:15–24; 16:19–31. See also
James 2:1–9; 5:1–6.

Theme: Those who have the spirit of the poor; those who do
not worry about tomorrow; those who hunger and thirst for justice; the merciful; those who are persecuted for the cause of
justice—all those are blessed and will inherit the Kingdom.
Those who remain indifferent, who do not place themselves at
the service of the needy, will be cursed.
Readings: Matt. 5:3–9; 6:25–34; 25:31–46. See also James
2:14–17; 4:13–17; 1 John 3:17–18.

Theme: One should not pile up riches on earth, for they will
only decay. Where one's wealth is, there also is one's heart. One
cannot serve God and money (the idol Mammon). Accumulated
wealth is stolen from the poor.
Readings: Matt. 6:19–24; Luke 12:13–34; 16:1–15. See also
James 4:13–5:6; Col. 3:5; Eph. 5:5; 1 Tim. 6:6–12, 17–19.

Theme: It will be difficult for those who are rich to enter the
Kingdom of God.
Reading: Mark 10:17–30.

(ii) Summary. Jesus realistically shows that the rich obses-
sively seek their opulent living and security by means of eco-

nomic success and selfish accumulation of goods. He sees a
possessive individualism in them, a concern for taking care of
only themselves. In them—besides any formal admission of
being rich and any religious practice associated with riches—he
denounces worship of a vain idol: Mammon, or the god money.
This is a real, actual form of worship, in which one's very life is
at stake, and an idolatrous, deceitful and empty worship, since
it leads to the "loss" of one's own life. Such idolatry is absolutely
incompatible with serving the true God and places a great obstacle in the way of God's coming Reign. It not only corrupts the
relationship between human beings and the goods of the earth
and leads to the loss of one's own life; it also vitiates relationships among people and degrades the life of the human community, leading us to despise others and oppress the poor. This
religion of the rich implies a false sense of superiority and self-
sufficiency, insensitivity and indifference to the deprivations and
sufferings of "our own flesh and blood." Selfishly accumulated
riches are the fruit of exploiting the poor, and so the god Mammon not only proves mortal to the rich, but also death-dealing
to the impoverished.

   The living and life-giving God, the God of the Kingdom and
its justice, has to be sought and served in the opposite direction
from the god of the rich and satisfied. The God of the coming
Kingdom, that of true joy, is the God of the poor: of those who
are now downtrodden and hungry (Luke), of those who, like the
Master, opt for the poor and side with the cause of the Kingdom,
entrusting their lives into the Father's hands (Matthew). They,
those who are unjustly relegated to a diminished life, those who
know how to share and risk their own lives . . ., receive life in
abundance from God, are the chosen ones of the Father's liberating love, are those destined to enjoy the Kingdom now and
inherit its future fullness.

(b) The God of the Kingdom, Opposed to the God of the Powerful

(i) Reading Guide
Theme: Christ comes to free the oppressed from the power
of the dominators.
Readings: Luke 1:46–55, 67–79; 4:14–21.

Theme: Behind the dominators stands the prince of this world, the power of darkness, the tempter.
Readings: Luke 4:5–8; 20:20–26; 22:39–53; John 12:31–33; 14:30. See also Eph. 6:10–13.

Theme: The governors oppress the people. Among those who follow Jesus, it must be otherwise: the first has to be a slave to the lesser and the last.
Readings: Matt. 20:20–28; Luke 22:24–30; John 13:1–7.

Theme: There are contradiction and opposition between the Kingdom of God and the kingdom (oppressive power) of this world, manipulated by Satan.
Readings: John 18:28–19:37. See also Rev. 13:1–18.

Theme: There are contradiction and opposition between the peace of Christ and the pax romana.
Readings: Luke 1:79; 2:14; John 14:27.

Theme: Christ is victor over the world, and the disciples are victors over fear.
Readings: John 16:1–11, 32–33; Matt. 10:17–31. See also Acts 4:23–31; Rev. 13:1–13; 19:11–12.

Theme: Before the Kingdom arrives in fullness, the imperial power retains a certain validity.
Readings: Mark 12:13–17; John 19:10–11. See also Rom. 13:1–7; 1 Pet. 2:13–17; Acts 4:19–20; 5:27–32.

(ii) Summary. Jesus does not situate his ministry on the same level as political power, nor in competition with it, and avoids direct confrontation with the authorities. But he acts with sovereign freedom in relation to them, and very clearly points to the ruling order and hierarchy as an order of domination, keeping the people in subjection. In the ruling military and political power, and in the religious authorities who comply with it, he denounces methods of murderous violence and lying ideology, on the part of those who unjustly require religious obedience from the people and impose themselves through fear. And behind the powers and authorities that subject the humble people, Jesus recognizes the empire of the "prince of this world."

The Kingdom that comes with Jesus, his own messianic kingship, "is not of this world": it has a different source and character, other aims and other means. Jesus' God is not the god of the ruling powers, not the "almighty" evoked and invoked by the powerful of this world, but precisely the opposite. His is the God who comes to reign, whose will is to be done . . . from the side of the weak, lifting up the downtrodden, setting captives free. Jesus himself, faithful to this God, does not seek to impose himself through force of arms, does not give in to the temptation to manipulate the masses through sacred symbols of power; he brings the justice that restores life, the truth that makes us free, the faith that gives victory over fear. The God of the Kingdom who comes with Jesus is none other than his Father, who comes to give us life and dignity, beginning with the most deprived; who commits us to following Jesus in his task of liberating the oppressed and by his way of humble service.

(c) The God of the Suffering Servant, Opposed to the God of the Popular Messianism of the Zealots

(i) Reading Guide
Theme: Jesus' ministry arouses nationalist and triumphalist expectations in the people and the disciples. About these matters Jesus is evasive.
Readings: John 6:14–15; 12:12–19; Mark 10:35–40; Luke 24:19–21. See also Acts 1:6–8.

Theme: From the beginning to the end of time, there is a (Satanic) temptation to messianic liberation through supernatural power or force of arms.
Readings: Luke 4:1–13; 9:51–56; 22:39–53; Matt. 26:51–54.

Theme: The disciples (Peter) define the Messiah, and Jesus does so also.
Reading: Mark 8:27 – 9:1.

Theme: Love for one's enemies and non-violent action are keys in the new Law of the Sermon on the Mount.
Readings: Matt. 5:3–12, 21–26, 38–48; Luke 6:27–38.

Theme: The question of Jesus' kingship arises in the trial before Pilate, and the meaning of his kingship is revealed on the cross.
Reading: John 18:28 – 19:37.

(ii) Summary. The "God" of Jewish hope at the time of Jesus had a large content of nationalist ideology — and that was not the last time in history "God" would be so used. In conflicts within society, "God" can be invoked by both sides, waging a holy war, demonizing the enemy as totally evil, promoting holy hatred and exterminating vengeance, even inspiring a mysticism of dying and killing for the cause. In the popular messianism surrounding Jesus there was the subversive movement of the Zealots, cruelly repressed by the authorities "as an example," but continually reasserting itself with a fair measure of influence over the people. They saw "God" as the apocalyptic avenger, worker of miracles and dealer of disasters, who would set Israel free from Roman dominion and give it a future of national greatness and religious prominence among the nations of the earth.

Jesus took care to distance himself from this movement, and on several occasions reprimanded his disciples for persisting in this type of expectation and acting in accordance with it. He pointed out that such expectations were inspired not by God, but by "another spirit," by Satan, the tempter. But he himself admitted to being tempted in this direction — his only such admission — and the Gospel narratives provide ample evidence that choosing his alternative course took a whole process of discernment and human maturing. This alternative, which progressively and ever more radically defined his messianic strategy and his very witness to God, was liberation through the way of humble service, in reference to the figure of the martyr-prophet hymned by Deutero-Isaiah. His is the strategy that relies on the strength of truth and justice, that trusts in the power of love even for enemies and persecutors; in this strategy one risks oneself for truth and struggles for justice through "non-violent" means, even risks and gives up one's own life. In this fashion, Jesus opened up the way of the cross to his disciples, showing them the confrontation with the mystery of God in the crucified Messiah, the definitive meeting with the God who raised the crucified Jesus from among the dead.

(d) The God of Mercy and Life, Opposed to the God of the Scribes and Pharisees, and of the Temple

(i) Reading Guide
Theme: Jesus cures the sick and forgives sins; he mixes in bad company; his disciples pick ears of grain on the sabbath; he breaks religious rules for the needy. The Pharisees are scandalized and look for ways of getting rid of him.
Readings: Mark 2:1–3:12; Luke 8:1–3.

Theme: The Pharisees criticize Jesus for mixing in bad company. Jesus explains his behaviour: "Who among you, if he has a hundred sheep and loses one . . .? What woman, if she has ten pieces of silver . . .? There was a man with two sons. The younger said to his father: 'Give me my share. . . .' "
Reading: Luke 15:1–32.

Theme: Publicans and prostitutes will go into the Kingdom before the priests, scribes and Pharisees.
Readings: Matt. 21:28–31; 5:20; Luke 7:36–50; John 8:2–11; Luke 18:9–14.

Theme: Jesus tells a teacher of the Law that the way to live is to follow these guidelines: "You shall love the Lord your God with all your heart . . . and your neighbour as yourself." And who is my neighbour? Jesus answer this question with the parable of the good Samaritan.
Reading: Luke 10:25–37.

Theme: It is no use making offerings, saying "Lord, Lord," being prominent in the community . . . without forgiving one's brothers and sisters and acting with justice.

Readings: Matt. 5:23–24; 7:21–23; Luke 13:22–30. See also James 1:26–27.

Theme: Jesus offers only woe to the "teachers of the Law and Pharisees, you hypocrites"; he does this because they have laid heavy burdens on others, have sought the prime positions for themselves, have sought to be called "master" and "father," have carried out the most minute observances of the Law while not fulfilling what is really important: justice, mercy and faith.
Readings: Mark 12:38–40; Matt. 23:1–36.

Theme: The leaders of the Jews seek to arrest Jesus, but they fear the people. He is a cause of division. Only those who are of God know him. The high priests and Pharisees despise the people as "sinners who do not know the Law," but they are not of God, but of the devil, who has been a liar and murderer from the beginning. Jesus gives true witness and gives "signs" that bring life (healing the paralytic, making the blind man see, raising Lazarus), but the high priests and Pharisees agree to deceive the people and have Jesus put to death.
Readings: John 7:11 – 11:54; 15:18–25. See also 1 John 1:5 – 2:11; 3:8–15.

(ii) Summary. The religious life and structure of Palestinian Judaism at the time of Jesus were divided between two strands of leadership: that of the priesthood, more aristocratic and conservative, tied to the centralized worship in the Temple with the economic power this brought; and that of the scribes and Pharisees, more popular and nationalistic, linked to teaching the Law in the liturgy of the synagogues – "base chapels" in small towns and villages. The Gospel narratives show Jesus most frequently and deeply in conflict with the power and authority of the latter group, who were closer to the daily lives of people and probably more oppressive. The scribes and Pharisees were learned teachers and formed pious confraternities – they were "pastors" and "religious" who looked after and taught the people. Jesus saw their practices, especially the religious and moral discipline they sought to impose on the people, as a formalistic degradation and corruption of biblical faith. The God of the covenant, who

elected through love, called and set free, had been turned into
a "God of the Law," demanding a mass of "observances" and
handing out judicial punishment, alienating and oppressing the
humble people.

Their "God" had become a judge, requiring and watching
over an endless series of prohibitions and commandments,
taboos and religious observances, bad things to avoid and good
deeds to be multiplied ... all written down in "his book" and
meriting reward or punishment in due measure, in this life or
the next. In this way, the relationship with the living God, who
loves and acts freely in human history, forgiving and liberating
completely and hoping for human response "from the heart,"
had been downgraded into a cold moralism of immanent justice.
In proud pretension, the religious officials saw themselves as
accumulating merit in God's eyes to a degree unattainable by
most people, and degraded a dynamic relationship with God
into a ritualism of religious observances motivated by fear or
petty self-interest.

Here Jesus' criticism applies to the ritualistic worship in the
Temple as well, following a long history in Israel's prophetic
tradition: "For it is love that I desire, not sacrifice; it is knowledge of God, not burnt offerings" (Hos. 6:6); "See the fast that
pleases me: to break the fetters of injustice ..., to set the
oppressed free. ... Fast by sharing your food with the hungry"
(Isa. 58:6–7). Jesus is here criticizing a "sacral" god, living in a
separate "religious world," apart from ordinary daily life, and
the castes of consecrated specialists in holiness; he is attacking
a "hierarchical" god, accessible to the people only through the
mediation of these castes, who hold the monopoly of religious
knowledge and sacred power.

Jesus' witness to God stands out with all the force of its
polemic when seen against this socio-cultural and religious background. As we have seen – in chapter IV, section 1c – Jesus was
born and lived as a lay person, concerned directly with the common people, showing them God's love and their responsibility
for the coming Kingdom directly, not through religious language
or "symbols." His "signs" were not ritual gestures, but human
ones, healing and saving men and women suffering from poverty,
alienation and demonic oppression. He put all religious prac-

tices and observances in their proper place: for the sake of health and a worthy life. He taught his disciples to recognize the presence of the risen Lord and the Father's love, not in the Temple rites or in solitary contemplation, but in their suffering fellow human beings, in the living community of their brothers and sisters.

The God of Jesus of Nazareth, then, is most clearly the God of humble and simple people, not of the wise and prudent. The most radical revelation of his God is as the God of forgiveness, as the Father who takes most joy in forgiving and giving life, who looks for a "heartfelt" response from us, given "with all our heart," before God and for our brothers and sisters. In the succinct phrases of John's Gospel, his God is the God of life and truth, as opposed to the God of the scribes and Pharisees, who is "a murderer and liar from the beginning." His is the God of daily, "secular" life, with its most material joys and sorrows; the God of the little, simple people, "those sinners who are ignorant of the Law."

4. JESUS' WITNESS AS SON

The God of the Kingdom, we have seen, is none other than the Father of Jesus Christ. The God who comes to "reign" on our earth through the historical ministry and paschal destiny of Jesus of Nazareth is none other than his own Father, whose way of acting and personal intimacy Jesus "knows" as no one else does, since he is "the beloved Son." This most radically personal dimension of Jesus' witness to God and his religious experience — their "filial" dimension — forms the heart of his witness to the God of the Kingdom.

To examine this dimension, we need to follow the main stages of the revelation Jesus conferred on his closest followers, as those stages appeared to the early Christian community and in particular to the compilers of the Gospels, following with them the development of the disciples' faith as they kept company with Jesus along his journey "beginning with John's baptism until the day when Jesus was taken away from us" (Acts 1:22).[3] I propose to examine five decisive stages on this journey: (a) the Sermon on the Mount; (b) Jesus' inner experience; (c) the road to the passion; (d) Jesus' death; (e) Easter and Pentecost. These steps in the Gospel story can perhaps show us the root of the living logic of our own journey in faith in the God of Jesus Christ, as we make this journey along the stony road of our own history.

(a) The Sermon on the Mount

Chapters 5 to 7 of Matthew's Gospel give us a collection of Jesus' sayings presented as the inaugural discourse of his public ministry. This discourse is not concerned with a supernatural world, nor—directly—with God's "supernatural" action in this world. It deals rather with this world of ours, with the basic matter of our everyday lives: sorrows and joys, working to feed and clothe ourselves, poverty and riches, domestic relationships, injustice and solidarity in dealing with friends and neighbours, judging and forgiving one's enemies.... All this brings us the incredible news that God cares about these concerns of ours, as a solicitous and infinitely capable parent.

Jesus' tone is not that of a "holy innocent." He knows that God can allow us to go hungry, suffer hatred and persecution, die. Furthermore, he proclaims those who suffer and are persecuted "fortunate." How can we reconcile this with his call for filial trust without limit? It is not that God wants hunger and tears; the tears Jesus calls "fortunate" are those God comes to wipe away. Jesus is not calling us to resign ourselves to, still less rejoice in, the suffering and injustice that fill the world. He tells us that the hour has come to rejoice because the Father has taken note of the destitution and exploitation his children are suffering from (cf. Exod. 3:7–8); he calls us to eradicate poverty and oppression from among us, because the true God wills that they should be done away with.

Jesus, then, is showing us God's loving attention to the lives of each one of us, particularly of the poor and vulnerable. That this is "shown" to us does not mean the veil of "another world" is being drawn aside, but that we are made to feel God's mysterious and saving presence in the centre of our own lives, in the heart of the world and among the poor and marginalized of the earth. We are shown God taking our lives and the world as they are, with their noblest expressions and desires, their base weight of selfishness, cruelty and death, and deciding on the radical liberation of creation.

Naturally, this interpretation of our lives and history in relation to God and liberation is not the only possible one. We might ask: If it is true that there is a God like this, could this God not have prevented all suffering and injustice from the outset? When Jesus could not hold back his tears before his friend's tomb, "The Jews said, 'See how he loved him!' But some of them said, 'If he could open the eyes of the blind man, could he not have saved this man from dying?' " (John 11:35–37).

So faith is a conscious choice. It is opting to give meaning to our lives, not to wander lost through a hostile world and end in nothingness; it is deciding that the sufferings and most secret hopes of the poor are not in vain; it is stating that each one of us has a truly fruitful task to perform in this world, and that human beings have a future of solidarity and love before them. It is a choice made for good reasons, but against good reasons too, and flying in the face of many absorbing and mystifying facts.

(b) Jesus' Inner Experience

Is such a choice, implying confidence in everything good in the world, a pure "toss of a coin"? If so, how can this be reconciled with the certainty proper to faith? In reality, the solid basis for such an option lies in the fact that it was Jesus who pronounced the Sermon on the Mount. Its power does not stem from an inner logic, nor from its inherent probability, nor from its consoling effect as religious discourse, but from the fact that it portrays the experience of Jesus himself: authentically human experience, of our life and our death, and inner experience of God as Father.

The Sermon on the Mount gives us the words of someone who lived what he said, and said what he lived. He himself experienced the harshness of the rich, hatred and persecution from enemies; every day as he went about, he met people who were hungry and in distress, and made them his companions and friends; he could see straight through hypocrisy and insincerity at first glance. He knew the Father's loving look on all this misery, and reacted to it like the Father.

Jesus lived the life he described in his words: a life spent entirely in the great cause of humankind, which is God's cause; he was threatened and attacked and lived a life of poverty in the firm and certain conviction of being in the Father's hands. Jesus' whole life showed this inner certainty that nothing could separate him from the Father's love, and he invites us to share this certainty, trusting in his experience as Son.

In the Gospel tradition, Jesus' life is dominated by his consciousness of having a unique relationship with God his Father. The first and last words recorded of his life on earth both refer to the Father (Luke 2:49; 23:46), and "No one knows the Son except the Father, and no one knows the Father except the Son and those to whom the Son chooses to reveal him" (Matt. 11:27; see 21:37; 24:36; cf. John 1:18; 10:15; 17:1–8, 20–26). This "knowing" is complete openness, unlimited confidence and total commitment, "revealed" precisely to "simple people" and to those "who work hard and who carry heavy burdens" (Matt. 11:25, 28). And Jesus' prayer, as attested in the Gospels, is usually one that in the most difficult or tragic situations expresses unlimited confidence in the Father's love; his innermost wish is that "thy will be done."[4] So, on the threshold of the passion, Mark (14:36) relates the fact — unheard-of in Jewish piety — that Jesus addressed God as "Abba," the Aramaic word used by children to their fathers in the bosom of the family.[5] It is the same word that — in the Spirit of Christ — Christians "dare" to use when they call on "Our Father" (see Rom. 8:15; Gal. 4:6; cf. Matt. 6:9; Luke 11:2; John 20:17). In doing so, they express the same shared experience that "neither life nor death . . ., neither the present nor the future, nor cosmic powers, were they from heaven or from the deep world below . . ., will separate us from the love of God, which we have in Jesus Christ, our Lord" (Rom. 8:38–39).

(c) The Road to the Passion

The Gospels present Jesus' public life in two distinct parts: the time of miracles and discourses, and the road to the passion.

In the first period, Jesus welcomes the poor, heals the sick and proclaims the coming of the Kingdom of God. The multiplication of loaves, with Jesus' great popular acclaim, marks the culmination of this first period (John 6:14–21). But he removes himself from popular enthusiasm, and retires alone, by night. There has in fact been a deep misunderstanding: the people have seized only on the promissory aspects of his message — abundance and reconciliation throughout the world — taking them for a populist messianism, a great sharing-out of happiness, a great miracle to take the place of human commitment and hard work. It is the same misunderstanding that has been the great "temptation" to his messianism from the beginning (see Matt. 4:1–11). It is true that the good news of God's Reign is good news of God's peace and plenty for the human race, but Jesus knows that God's peace and plenty do not change the structures of the world by magic, nor are they offered without our humble acceptance and generous commitment. And the world in which the good news has to be proclaimed is a world in which we have multiplied poverty, have institutionalized contempt for and despoiling of our neighbours: a world in which those who give themselves to the cause of justice have to know hatred and persecution, in which those who believe in God cannot exempt themselves from darkness, failure and death.

For us to go on believing in the Father in the depths of suffering, humiliation and failure, Jesus had to plumb the depths of human misery. He had to know all the abandonment, hatred and cruelty that human beings can inflict on one another: betrayal and persecution, humiliating interrogation and torture, the horrible death by crucifixion. Without this, his forgiveness would be simply turning his back on the human condition, his proclamation of the beatitudes a mere golden dream, an alienating illusion.

After the multiplication of the loaves, Jesus brutally tore his disciples out of this dream. He removed them from the enthusiasm of the crowd and left them alone on the night of the storm. This shows that faith is not just latching on to Jesus as saviour and staying close to him. It is also doing what he requires of us when he is absent: going on believing in the truth, struggling for justice and living in love, in times of lies, selfishness and exploitation. So, when Peter confessed his faith in Jesus as "the Christ" — the saviour sent by God in whom we can put all our trust — Jesus' reply made him understand the full implications of this confession: he would have to suffer and those who want to follow Jesus have to take up their cross.

Putting ourselves in the Father's hands when life stretches ahead of us full of promise, when everyone is smiling on us and we can see the fruits of our labours growing, is easy enough and can be pure illusion. It is when the future is cloudy and all our props have been removed that we can learn with Jesus to trust in the Father alone. This will be asked of us in all its force when we come to die, but it is also true that loneliness and death are with us to some extent throughout our lives. This is why the Gospels show Jesus, some months before his death, teaching his disciples to follow him with the cross of "subversives" condemned to death.

(d) Jesus' Death

Jesus made his solemn affirmation of his full messianic dignity (Mark 14:61–62) only when he found himself bound and powerless before the authorities of the land, judged an abject being whose elimination was necessary for national security (see John 11:45–54). His cruel and humiliating death, abandoned by everyone, came as an ironic denial of all his claims, a violent abortion of all the hopes the people had put in him: "They struck him saying, 'Play the prophet!' " (Mark 14:65) . . . "Jesus the Nazarene, King of the Jews" . . . "Let the King of Israel now come down from his cross and we will believe in him. He trusted in God: if God loves him, then he will save him, since he himself said: 'I am Son of God' " (Matt. 27:42–43).

Jesus experienced to extreme degree the abandonment and impotence of death, seeing the great cause that had been the driving force of his life in ruins. In this human failure and death, only the Son of God could remain unshakeably sure of his Father. By dying in the Father's hands, Jesus radically conquered all the despairs and scepticisms that darken our lives and paralyze our struggles for a better world: he radically conquered all the unbelief that threatens us in our human nature, founding a faith stronger than death.

Jesus experienced the very worst that our human nature can produce: cowardice, treachery, petty ambition, cruelty. Such human rejection and abjectness could be forgiven only by the Son of God; he alone could remain unshakeably attached to a human race that had unanimously agreed to get rid of him: Jews and Romans, rich and poor, people and authorities. By dying for the sake of his enemies, Jesus radically conquered all the prejudices, wars and divisions that tear the human race apart, and founded a human community that is stronger than death.

In such an extreme situation, only the Son of God was capable of continuing to call God "my Father," and others "my brothers and sisters." It is just here that Jesus' divinity becomes clear: in this radical certainty, which did not protect him in the least from the harshness of life, the cruelty of men, the loneliness of death ... but which transforms all these into a witness to the unshakeable love that binds him to his Father and to us.

Jesus' violent death, therefore, is essential for giving our Christian faith its full breadth and depth. It is only in his passion that Jesus shows us just how far it is possible to live the Sermon on the Mount: blind trust in the Father and love for one's enemies. Only there does he show us that the beatitudes remain valid to the extremes of poverty, of thirst for justice, of persecution. Jesus' death, in the most complete despoilment and rejection, was necessary to assure us that God's faithfulness can never fail us. In Jesus Christ the Son, our faith in the God of love and life has become unshakeable.

(e) Easter and Pentecost

It was a fact, nevertheless, that at the time of Jesus' passion, the faith of his disciples was violently shaken, scandalized, if not completely eradicated. He who had been hailed as the great prophet of the people was dying alone and abandoned, and his scattered disciples saw his death as the end of all the hopes they had felt burgeon as they followed him.

It was only their meeting with the risen Jesus—an unheard-of and unhoped-for experience—that gave the disciples some

idea of the victory he owed to his Father beyond death. Their
experience of the risen Jesus showed the disciples not just that
Jesus was alive after death. Above all it meant that Jesus really
was what he had claimed to be for the people, and had now
come to be that with an undreamt-of fullness; that Jesus' cause
was still valid, and had already won its decisive victory for the
liberation of the people and of all human beings; that the Sermon on the Mount had been totally vindicated; that the God of
Jesus really was—beyond all doubt—the Father of all; and that
Jesus' fellow men and women, whom he had made his "neighbours"—beyond all enmity—really were all brothers and sisters
and had to come together as God's family.

Christ's pasch, however, as objective basis of faith, was not a
purely external event for the disciples. It was not just the great
"argument for" faith, but the source of faith as new energy and
irrepressible dynamism. The creator of all life had made Jesus
raised from among the dead become the principle of a new life,
communicated to his followers through faith. In New Testament
terms, the risen Jesus poured out the power of his Spirit on his
followers, the Spirit of his new life, of his victory, the Spirit who
made him live as the Son of God and brother of all human
beings. This mysterious reality, the "contagion" of Christ's
pasch, was what Luke was describing in his account of the Pentecost event (Acts 2).

For those who believed in the risen Christ, the experience of
the Spirit meant that Jesus was definitively with them, and that
these groups of believers were now the community or "church"
of Christ. It meant that the God of Jesus of Nazareth, who raised
Jesus crucified, was—beyond doubt—the God of those who
believe in Christ. It meant that these believers were the "brothers and sisters" of Jesus Christ and could with this same Spirit
call God "Abba," "Our Father" (see Matt. 6–7; Rom. 8; John
20). It meant that these communities now made up the new
people of God: a prophetic people, called to carry on Jesus'
public ministry among all the peoples of the earth, bearing witness, in words and deeds, to the one living and true God . . . so
that God's Kingdom may come and all may have life (see 1
Thess. 1; 1 Cor. 1; Matt. 28; Acts 1–2; John 20; 1 John 1–3).

CHAPTER VII

God in the New Testament Message

1. EXPERIENCE OF GOD IN THE NEW TESTAMENT

In our more or less secularized urban culture, what is likely to strike us in reading the New Testament is the uncomplicated spontaneity with which it treats "knowledge" of God. With our more critical mentality, we are conscious of the ambiguity of all religious experience and need to reflect, to a greater or lesser degree, on the way we know God. In more "enlightened" circles, it is even necessary to make a critical assessment of the bases for affirming the existence of God. The people portrayed in the New Testament have no such problem: for them, God exists; that is the first thing. Their problem is never to discover whether God exists, but to learn how God acts among people. Their reflection does not start by analyzing the world and everyday life in order to find a "beyond" or a "deep down" of mystery and absoluteness; it starts from an unquestioned acceptance of the living God, inquiring into the nature of the human condition and the meaning of history in relation to this God.

The New Testament accepts that "the power and divinity" of the one God can be known by starting from the world (see Rom. 1:19–20); it also recognizes that trying to find God in a metaphysical quest for the basis of life itself is hard work, a process of "groping" (Acts 17:27). But the real basis for the understanding of God that people have in the New Testament does not rely on this type of metaphysics.

Another striking fact is that this unquestioning knowledge of God is not in the least weakened by experience of the extreme ignorance of God shown by the surrounding pagan world, of which the New Testament is well aware (besides Rom. 1 and Acts 17, see 1 Thess. 4:5; 2 Thess. 1:18; 1 Cor. 1:21; Gal. 4:8; Eph. 1:12; 4:18). For the early Christians, such nonknowledge of God is always a fault in itself, or punishment for a fault: it is a disowning, directly or indirectly willed, on the part of those who "walk in darkness," of people who have fallen into idolatrous absolutization of a world dominated by the spirits of evil, enemies of God and of divine justice (see Acts 14:15; 17:29; 1 Thess. 1:9; 1 Cor. 8:1–7; 12:12; Gal. 4:3, 9; Rom. 1:21–23; Col. 2:8, 18–20; Eph. 4:12, 17–18).

For the New Testament Christians, taking their message to the pagans does not have to involve lengthy explanations of a divine reality hitherto unsuspected by them; they simply have to tell them of the saving intervention of a God whom they already, deep down, know. It is just that they have not been willing to accept this profound truth of the one God; they hide it from themselves under pretext of an apparently self-satisfied notknowing. So the decisive argument the New Testament preachers use for conversion from idolatry to the living God is not metaphysical argument about what seems a self-evident truth, but the proclamation of this God's new action in the passion and resurrection of Jesus Christ (see 1 Thess. 1:4–10; 1 Cor. 1:18ff; 15:3ff; Acts 17:31). By proclaiming this "good news," they are at the same time "uncovering" previous knowledge of God which the pagans had covered over with sin.

The basis of this evidence or spontaneous knowledge of God shown by New Testament Christians is the simple but monumental fact that God is revealed to them, made clear to them, through divine action in history. In the first place, as Jews, they were convinced that the living God is shown in the history of their people: "God has spoken in the past to our fathers, through the prophets, in many different ways" (Heb. 1:1). And this same God "of [their] fathers," the God "of Abraham, Isaac and Jacob," is their God, the self-appointed God of their nation, who has acted with it throughout history (see Stephen's speech in Acts 7:2–53, and Paul's in Antioch, in Acts 13:16–41).

But it is not only through hearsay, through accounts of God's actions in the past of their nation, that the New Testament Christians know about God; they have experienced the living reality of God through the new divine intervention in the history they have been part of. In the first place: God has spoken "definitively to us through his Son" (Heb. 1:2), shown his saving grace through his Son (Tit. 2:11); the only Son has spoken to them of the God no one has ever seen (John 1:18): he, the Word of life, whom they have seen with their eyes, heard with their ears, touched with their hands (1 John 1:1–3). In the second place: God is making them feel the divine presence now—the saving presence of the risen Christ—through the action of the Spirit: charisms, joy, the "parousia" . . . in the midst of conflicts and persecutions. (These two aspects have clear trinitarian resonances for us now, but the first Christians could not see them in this way. For them the action of the Spirit did not reveal the "person" of the Holy Spirit, but the lordship of Christ "spiritually" present in his church. It was a matter of two different ways of experiencing Jesus: "according to the flesh," and "according to the Spirit" [see Acts 1:21ff; 10:41; 1 Cor. 9:1; 12:3; 2 Cor. 5:16]).

New Testament believers, then, felt an indissoluble unity between their knowledge of God and their experience of Jesus Christ. This is expressed in innumerable formulas in which God and Jesus Christ appear together: conversion to the living and true God goes with hoping for his Son's second coming (1 Thess. 1:9–10); salvation, eternal life, consists in "communion" with the Father and the Son (1 John 1:3), in "knowing" the true God and the one that God has sent (John 17:3). And these two realities are not simply juxtaposed: their union is so close in faith experience that abandoning one also excludes the other: "He who denies the Son is without the Father" (1 John 2:23).

It is true that the New Testament also shows a valid knowledge of God without faith in the Son. But faced with the fact and personality of Jesus, in the situation of urgency created by God's intimation to us through the incarnate Word, rejecting Jesus Christ amounts in practice to not knowing God. So the leaders of the Jews who reject Jesus, though they call on the God of their fathers, in fact do not know God (see John 8:42, 54–55).

To sum up: the New Testament shows the faith of the believers of the early church centred on their clear and intense experience of Jesus Christ as a living and tangible reality, of the memory of his deeds and words, his public life and his fate, and his actual presence through the action of the Spirit. This experience, the centre and whole of their lives, is the place where they meet God. Jesus Christ is for them the living sacrament of God, a sacrament that has transformed them through its action, "converted" them to a new "knowledge" of the living God and a new, vital and joyous intimacy with that God. This is the beginning and end of their knowledge of God: not a brilliant exposition of their religious sense, nor a philosophical concept they have had to "grope" for, but the self-revelation of God through grace in Jesus Christ.

2. THE ONE GOD

Jesus himself, in the decisive context of being asked which was the most important commandment, made the traditional Jewish confession of monotheistic faith his own: "Hear, Israel! The Lord, our God, is one Lord; and you shall love the Lord, our God, with all your heart" (Mark 12:28ff). Though often expressed in Old Testament formulas, confession of the one God runs through the whole of the New Testament as part of its basic message. When Paul sums up what it means to have become Christians, he tells the Thessalonians that it is first conversion to the living and true God (1 Thess. 1:9). For John, eternal life consists in "knowing" and "glorifying" this one true God (John 5:44; 17:3). The Epistles reiterate that "there is one [only] God" (*heis ho Theos* [Rom. 3:30; 1 Cor. 8:6; Gal. 3:20; Eph. 4:6; 1 Tim. 2:5; James 2:19]), and "[one] God alone" (*monos Theos* [Rom. 16:27; 1 Tim. 1:17; 4:15; Jude 25; Rev. 15:4]). Even the expression "good news of God" often seems to have the sense of proclaiming the one true God (as in 1 Thess. 2:2, 8, 9; Rom. 15:16). Paul bases two of his central ideas on the fact that God is one: the call to the gentiles as part of the one people of the new covenant (Rom. 3:28–30; 10:2; 1 Tim. 2:4–5), and the unity of the various spiritual activities in the one body of Christ (1 Cor. 12:16; Eph. 4:6).

This New Testament profession of monotheism does not — as we have seen — refer to a more or less obvious metaphysical presupposition, that of an original and final unity beyond the multiplicity of the world. The one God is certainly said to be the *fons et origo* of all being and all life (see 1 Cor. 8:6; 12:6; Acts 17:25, 28), and this ontological relationship makes it possible to "discover" God through the world (Rom. 1:20). But profession of faith in the one God is based not on knowledge of the single origin and end of the world, but on this "good news of God." It is not a "metaphysical," but a "prophetic" monotheism that the New Testament expresses.

This monotheism is not a neutral statement, either; it is a profession of faith against those "many gods and lords" that exist in the world (1 Cor. 8:5–6). Many powers act in and dominate the world — human powers, and diabolical ones behind them — but Christians recognize, as the one God and Lord, the living God who has acted and is acting in the Lord Jesus Christ and in the spiritual process of salvation that stems from him. The "one God" of Christians is specifically that living person who acted in the history of the Old Testament, and who is now active and fully revealed in Jesus Christ: the "God of our fathers" and the "God and Father of our Lord Jesus Christ" (Rom. 15:6; 2 Cor. 1:3; 11:31; Eph. 1:3, 17). As Karl Rahner said: "Those who profess one sole God without being willing to admit that this God is the God of the fathers and of our Lord Jesus Christ, are not speaking of the God confessed by the early church: 'Yet for us, there is but one God' (1 Cor. 8:6)."[1]

Nor is the fact that God is one understood in the New Testament as the merely ecstatic affirmation of a truth "in itself," but rather is understood as a reality that has to be imposed on the world and on history: God has to come to be the only God of the human race (see 2 Cor. 6:16; Heb. 8:10; Rev. 21:7). In this sense, the "Reign" of God is a seed planted in the world which has to germinate and grow throughout history till "God is all in all" (1 Cor. 15:24–28; see Mark 4:30–32).

It is precisely because the Kingdom has been given to the

disciples that for them professing their faith in the one God is not merely proclaiming a fact, but also a duty: that of the First Commandment, that of exclusive and total love of the one God, a love committed to spreading the fire that Christ came to bring to earth (see Luke 12:32, 49; Mark 12:28–34). Only in this love, of heart and arm, can we see if the one God is really the only God for those who confess their faith; if they are not serving some other lord or adoring some idol; if they are ready to serve God alone and give to God what is God's; if they are listening to God alone and building their lives on God's word; if they will be faithful to the end, even under the direst threats, and even if the end is martyrdom. And they have to be prepared to do all this, not just as one step that is taken once and for all, but as an ever-renewed "turning from idols to serve the living and true God."[2]

3. THE PERSONAL GOD

The knowledge New Testament Christians had of God was based on their experience of God as "someone" who had intervened in their history, who had sought to relate to them. The examples of Christian prayer found in the New Testament witness to this same personal aspect: God is someone who can be called "Thou," someone to converse with as between persons.

(a) God Acts Freely

Metaphysical knowledge of God certainly supposed that God, as "beginning and end" of all reality, acts; that the whole world is a result and sign of God at work. But this is seeing God's activity as absolutely, always and everywhere, transcendent, and therefore diffuse and anonymous in relation to human knowledge. The essence of biblical experience of God, on the other hand, is that it knows a determined and distinct action on God's part within the world and in a "here and now" perfectly differentiated from all others.

In the New Testament, therefore, the revelation of God in the world is not bound up with some uniform quality belonging to the whole of reality. God chose a particular nation, and to this alone gave "the covenants, the Law . . . and the promises" (Rom. 9:4). God sent God's Son to be born of this nation, at a specified time (Gal. 4:4), and on this — contingent and unique — event our salvation and the liberation of the world depend (see Acts 4:12; Rom. 8:18–30; Eph. 2:18).

God is of course present and active in saving and giving life, in universal history, in all nations and through all ages, but this is not something we can know automatically. The New Testament Christians knew this call to all nations to reconciliation and communion, not from some metaphysical learning about God's necessary goodness, but from faith in that "good news" of the great "mystery" hidden from the whole of humankind and "made known" at that time in Jesus Christ: that God, in the perfect freedom of a personal love that chooses and makes distinctions, now, unhoped-for and unexpectedly, offers salvation to all the nations and to all human beings (see Acts 2:17–18; Eph. 1–3).

This understanding of God's free and personal actions in history is what explains why faith in God as creator of the universe is so alive and immediate in the New Testament (see Matt. 11:25; Mark 13:19; John 1:3; Acts 4:24; 17:24; Rom. 11:36; 1 Cor. 8:5ff; Col. 1:15; Eph. 3:9; Heb. 1:2; 2:10; 3:4; 11:3; Rev. 4:11). These Christians see God as creator not in the world itself, but in God's self-revelation in the Word. The Israelites knew what "creating" was through their own experience of God's powerful and unconditional works in their own particular history. There they experienced in specific form that the living God is the one who "calls into being what does not exist" (Rom. 4:17 — referring, in its context, to God's free actions in the story of Abraham, but at the same time precisely expressing New Testament faith in the creator God).

God's sovereignty is exercised objectively over all the fortunes of the world, history, and the human race, since God is Lord, creator of heaven and earth (see Matt. 11:25; Acts 4:24ff; Eph. 1:11). But Christians experience God's creative power and absolute sovereignty over the world in the specific history of God's salvific interventions "here and now." Believers know God's "extraordinary power" through the raising of Christ from the dead (Eph. 1:19–20). This is specifically how they "know" that

"God disposes all things as he wills" (1:11). The basic facts of
our salvation in Jesus Christ are, then, what taught the New
Testament Christians to know God's always unforeseeable freedom, to recognize God acting in all other spheres—human life,
history, nature—with the same freedom.

As for our destiny, which is in the hands of this sovereign
Lord, we can trust confidently in the fidelity and truthfulness of
God, whose design for our salvation is irrevocable. (God is
"faithful" [*pistos*] in Rom. 3:3; 1 Cor. 1:9; 1 Cor 1:18; 2 Tim.
2:13; Heb. 10:23; 1 Pet. 4:19. God is "true," loyal [*alethes, ale-
thinos*], in Rom. 3:4; 15:8; John 3:33; 8:26.) But what the future
actions of God in our history, affecting our lives and our world,
will be, depends entirely on God's sovereignly free power, and
for us is a mystery that will be revealed only at the end of time.
We can never bring God within the grasp of our calculations:
God is and always will be Lord, taking pity on some and "hard-
ening the hearts" of others; and . . . "Who are you to call God
to account?" (see Rom. 9:15–20). We, in our lives as Christians,
must always take God's free and sovereign decision as the first
thing and the last.

(b) God Enters into Dialogue with Us

God acts in history with sovereign freedom. But if we experience God's action so intensely as personal, this is precisely
because God deals with us too as persons, because God's saving
action in history is directed to our hearts through the Word,
because God speaks to us "heart to heart." God, freely, enters
into an "I-thou" dialogue with us, inviting us to make an equally
free response.

Metaphysical reasoning starts from immediately experienced
reality and moves to an ultimate basis of reality, which it calls
God. It therefore always runs the risk of seeing the world as a
mere reflection of God, or of seeing God as simply the inner
key or meaning of the world. In other words, although metaphysics can come to know that God is personal, it almost inevitably brings the danger of failing to appreciate the reciprocal,
interpersonal relationship between God and ourselves.

The reality of this interpersonal relationship between God

and human beings, so hard to grasp metaphysically, is immediately obvious to believers throughout biblical history. There, God really challenges people, inviting them to enter freely into "conversation" with God, in an interpersonal relationship of friendship and collaboration. And the word God directs to people is one of true invitation—that is, the action of one person on another treated as such—not coercion—the action of one person on another treated as a thing. It is a true dialogue, in which people respond as they wish to the word addressed to them, even sometimes opposing themselves to God's proposal. They can "harden their hearts" (Rom. 2:5; Heb. 3:13), "resist the Holy Spirit" (Acts 7:51), obey God's will or not (Rom. 5:18; 16:19), close the door when the Lord knocks (Rev. 3:20) or set their own will against God's saving plan (Matt. 23:37ff). The very idea of spiritual beings opposed to God and divine justice, the very reality of sin with all its seriousness in God's eyes, as well as the invitation to repentance stemming truly from the heart of the sinner ... all merely confirm the importance of this double, interpersonal relationship between God and human beings.

God's action in history—we know from the biblical tradition—is neither paternalist nor populist, but a true liberating dialogue between God and people, through which God seeks to promote creatures to genuine familiarity and free collaboration. It is a dramatic dialogue, because God has given human beings the power to make their own response to God's word, with all the risk this implies: delays, backsliding, failure; this situation means that God's later words and actions really depend on that free human response.

This very real risk is the inevitable counterpart of God's purpose to take our human nature seriously, to hope for a response to divine love springing truly from human "hearts," like the love of a child for its parents, of one partner for another, not that of a servant or slave. In this sense, it is both true and false to say that everything in history proceeds from the will of God, which no one can contradict. Scripture shows the almighty God inviting creatures with free will to do what God wants; this is a true invitation, even though made by the one to whom all things are possible. God still retains the final word in history, not in the sense of using superior physical strength to violate the will of creatures, but rather in the sense that even the sinfulness of sinners, though entailing perdition for them, remains within the ambit of the absolute will of God and remains a means by which the divine love is to be glorified. In this way, God's power is shown even in the "vessels that deserved his wrath" (Rom. 9:22–23).

(c) The "Attributes" of the Divine Being

Seeing God as a transcendent person who enters into a dialogue with human beings in history gives us what the New Testament shows to be the right way of approaching the "essential attributes" of God.[3] In effect, if God is a living person who deals with us, the decisive aspect for us is not knowing what God is, but whom God wishes to appear as when intervening in our world and our history. This means that God, like all beings with whom we have personal relationships, does not so much show "attributes" as modes of action, "attitudes," freely and personally adopted.

It is true that these "attitudes" also show a coherence, a certain "structure" that reveals something of God's "essence." But these same attitudes, in their specific reality, do not necessarily spring from the divine essence. So God can show compassion or "harden his heart," enlighten or send the "power of delusion" (2 Thess. 2:11), without ceasing to be the holy one, whose judgments are true and just (Rev. 19:2). So the vital thing for us is not to know what God necessarily is, but what actual attitude God is in fact taking to us, how God is looking on our lives and fates, what our people actually mean to God.

So when the New Testament speaks of God as just, this implies an overwhelming impression of the holiness of God, the revelation of which forces us to a new and radical understanding of our sinfulness, of the fact that we are given over to wickedness (Rom. 1–3). This is seen in the terribly real and concrete fact of Jesus' death on the cross; there God "condemns the sin in this human condition," the condition of Christ, whom God made "bear our sin" (Rom. 8:3; 2 Cor. 5:21). But this experience of God's justice-dealing wrath does not mean that this is the necessary reaction of God's "essence" to the sin of the world. The same sin can also meet God's patience, just as this "time of patience" can be suddenly interrupted by God, who comes like a thief in the night (see Rom. 2:4; 3:26; 9:22; 1 Pet. 3:20; 2 Pet. 3:9–10; Matt. 24:37–44; Luke 12:16–21, 35–40).

The same can be said of the New Testament's speaking of God as good, or merciful. God is often said to forgive; God is merciful, generous, loving, the God of all grace and all consolation, the God of hope and peace, the God of love that wills the salvation of all. But this merciful love of God is shown to be essentially gratuitous, offered now beyond all hoping to a humankind "without God" (Eph. 2:12). So God's love for us is not a metaphysical "given," not a necessary "attribute" of the divine "essence." On the contrary, it is the great miracle, the astonishing fact above all, and the central object of the "good news," needing the special gift and humble acceptance of faith to understand it. As John would put it, the love of God had to "appear" in this world through the sending of God's Son, "that we might have life through him" (1 John 4:9); and we have known this love in the Word made flesh, and have believed in it (1 John 4:16).

For the New Testament, then, what matters is not some theoretical synthesis of the eternal attributes of God, but the historical account of the experience people and communities have had with God through meeting and following Jesus Christ.

4. THE GOD OF LOVE

The believers of the New Testament knew that the living God can act in different ways at various times. What was decisive in their faith and message, though, was to know that this holy God had in fact, freely and unforeseeably, willed to speak the last word in this dramatic dialogue between God and humankind: the word of saving love. More: the decisive experience of the Christians of the New Testament was that the God of their fathers has called us, in his Son and out of pure grace, to a salvation exceeding all human expectations: to the most intimate communion with God; God has called us to enjoy, in the most perfect human solidarity, the happiness that constitutes the very

life of God (see the prologues to John and 1 John; 1 John 4:7 –
5:13; Eph. 1:3–14). This experience is "definitive," and so we
need to see: (a) how it differs from God's actions in the Old
Testament; and (b) what its characteristics are.

a. The history of the Old Testament is made up of a series
of God's actions "at various times and in various different ways,"
whereas what happened "in our own time, the last days," is not
merely the last of a series; it is something new not only in relation to each of the earlier actions, but in relation to the whole
series. What happened "in our own time" is different from anything that happened earlier, but in the sense of being its goal
and consummation (*telos* and *pleroma*): that is, it is the "eschatological" intervention of God.

God is absolutely free and transcends the world and history;
God is infinite in possibilities of action and acts in such a way
as to impose no necessary conditions on subsequent actions.
Nevertheless, in the interests of self-definition, God has adopted
an approach to human beings and the world that cannot, by
God's own declaration, be changed or revoked. With this, the
inner history of the world has reached its final "conjuncture"
(its eschatological *kairos*), since the approach of the living God
experienced in the Christ-event is God's final and definitive contribution to the dialogue entered into with human beings, which
gives the history of the world its underlying meaning.

In the Old Testament, God deals personally with people,
showing them merciful goodness. But on the basis of the Old
Testament alone, we cannot finally say that this goodness indi-
cates God's love for humankind in the sense of seeking to share
the deepest intimacy of God's being, as between friends. Goodness, kindness, care . . . are also attitudes that can be shown by
master to servant, while the master himself remains distant and
inaccessible.

It is true that by intervening personally in history, the God
of the Old Testament was already in a way renouncing his inaccessible transcendence and committing himself to the world of
human beings. The deep meaning of this initiative on God's part
can be seen retrospectively from the New Testament, as a movement toward the bequest of God's personal intimacy to be made
in Jesus Christ, but this could not be seen from within the Old

Testament. This does not deprive the "faithful servants" of the old covenant from sharing the "joy of the master" (see Matt. 25:14–23): seeing themselves as mere servants, they were in fact children. But this was a promise to which they had to "look ahead and rejoice in from afar" (Heb. 11:13), till, in the fullness of time, God sent the Son to "show us the mystery" of the Father's plan of love for us (see Gal. 4:4; Eph. 1:3–10).

b. Saying that love is the decisive characteristic of God's dealings with us in these "last" days, then, means stating two things: (i) that this love of God given to us in Jesus Christ is an event, a free act on God's part, a happening, not a necessary "attribute" of the divine "essence"; (ii) that this same love is in fact offered to us in the form of full communion in the most intimate life of God.

These two elements are precisely what constitute the most authentic and personal love in our human experience. In the first place, love is not just the natural irradiation of a person, but the conscious and free giving of someone in full possession of himself or herself, and therefore able to give or not give, to open out or hold back in relation to another known, chosen, or accepted person. In the second place, love in its fully personal sense is not just some understanding relationship between two persons meeting in a third reality: a task, a truth, an ideal . . ., but an opening out and entrusting of one's deepest intimacy to the person loved.

And this is how God's love for us is shown in Jesus Christ:

i. Not as the prototype of a necessary and invariable procedure on God's part, but as a free offer which, even though it underlaid all God's actions in history, took shape fully and definitively only in the Christ-event. So much so, that God's love can be said to have "appeared" (Tit. 3:4) for the first time in this event; in this, "God showed his love for us" (Rom. 5:8) in this world. We know that God so loved the world from the unheard-of event of God's giving his only Son to the world (John 3:16; 1 John 4:9–10, 16). And this produced a definitive and irrevocable event, since Christ endures forever (see Heb. 6:17–20; 7:20–28; 10:5–14). Therefore, come what may, nothing "will separate us from the love of God, which we have in Jesus Christ, our Lord" (Rom. 8:39).

ii. What Christ has given us is nothing less than "communion" (*koinonia*) with the living God (see 1 John 1:3: in the demotic Greek of the time, *koinonia* meant marital relations). This "communion" is effectively established by the Spirit of Christ, who is none other than the Spirit of God through which God "pours out" personal love on us (see Rom. 5:5; Gal. 4:6; 1 John 3:24; 4:5). The most intimate personal life of God is opened up to us through the Spirit, because "the Spirit probes everything, even the depth of God" (1 Cor. 2:10–12). So the Spirit leads us into the most personal "knowledge" of God (see John 15:26; 16:13; 1 John 2:20–27). This is the Spirit that makes us "adopted children" and assures us that we really are "children of God" (Rom. 8:15–16), called to know God as God knows us (see Gal. 4:4, 6; 1 John 3:1–2; 1 Cor. 13:12). In this way, we are taken up into intimate communion of life with the God whom it is said no one has ever seen or can see (John 1:18; 1 Tim. 6:16), whom only the Son knows and reveals (see Matt. 11:27; John 3:11, 32; 7:29), enabling us to participate in his own joy and rights as Son (see Rom. 8:17, 29; Heb. 2:11–12).

So, saying that "God is love" (1 John 4:8, 16) is not making an obvious statement about the necessary essence of God; rather it expresses the unique experience believers had of God in Jesus Christ: that in the Son, the living God is given to us, wholly and irrevocably. And the immediate consequence, the concrete verification of this radical truth of the gospel, the only commandment of the new covenant, is not just that we in turn should love God, but that we should love one another: we should enter into that movement of God's love by ourselves loving—as Jesus did and with his same Spirit—our fellow beings, whose neighbours we must become, starting with those most in need and most oppressed. This is the constant message of the New Testament.

The Paradoxes of the God of Jesus Christ

1. The God of Jesus Christ is the God of a people and of history, the public God, the God of all, and at the same time, the God of the most personal intimacy, "my Father," whom "no one knows except the Son and those to whom the Son chooses to reveal him," the God of Jesus and of his "brothers and sisters" and friends.

2. The God of Jesus Christ is the Holy God, the transcendent "Lord of heaven and earth," radically different and absolute, to be loved "with all our heart and all our mind and all our will," the only yardstick by which our lives are to be judged. And at the same time, this is the "God-with-us," involved in our daily lives, attentive to our needs and joys as children of God.

3. The God of Jesus Christ is the God of past history, "of the fathers," and of the future fullness of the Kingdom that is to come, the God of tradition and of our ultimate hope. And at the same time, this is the God who comes to meet us today, asking us today to live in the presence of God and respond with concrete deeds.

4. The same God is the creator and universal Father, who makes no distinctions and "makes the sun shine on the good and the wicked." And at the same time, this is the God who loves with sovereign freedom, who chooses some in preference to others, who urges us to make a radical choice when faced

with God's love, a choice on which our salvation or perdition depends.

5. The God of Jesus Christ is the living and intensely personal God, whose love must be taken extremely seriously; the God who will not tolerate hypocrisy, frivolity or negligence, and who comes like a thief in the night. And at the same time, this is the God of merciful loving-kindness, who finds joy in the repentant sinner, who feasts the returning son.

6. This is the God who wills good things to God's children, the God who brings life in abundance, peace and joy. And at the same time this is the God of the poor and those who suffer, who "fills the hungry with good things and sends the rich away empty."

7. The God of Jesus Christ is the God of justice, of victory over the splintering and death-dealing power of sin. And by the same token, this is the God who is with the oppressed and marginalized, who takes the side of those who are persecuted, repressed and condemned by the kingdom of this world; this is the God who raised Jesus crucified, and who raises all those crucified in history.

Notes

PART ONE: THE GOD OF THE POOR

I. The Subject of God

1. In Greek, *ho theos* — with the article — is used to indicate *the* one God.

2. See St Thomas Aquinas, *S. Th.,* I, q.1, a. 3, 7.

3. See DV 12, 23–4; GS 44, 57–9, 62; AG 22. The subject was taken up more forcefully in relation to the Latin American context at the Second General Conference of Latin American Bishops at Medellín, Colombia, in 1968, and at the Third General Conference at Puebla, Mexico, in 1979. A pioneering work in this respect was J. L. Segundo, *Nuestra idea de Dios,* vol. 3 of *Teología abierta para el laico adulto* (Buenos Aires and Mexico, 1970). Eng. trans.: *Our Idea of God,* vol. 3 of *A Theology for Artisans of a New Humanity* (Maryknoll, N.Y., 1974).

4. See M. D. Chenu, *La théologie est-elle une science?* (Paris, 1957). Eng. trans.: *Is Theology a Science?* (London, 1959).

5. See M. Blondel, *L'action; essai d'une critique de la vie et d'une science de la pratique* (Paris, 1950); H. Bouillard, *Blondel et le Christianisme* (Paris, 1961); idem, *Connaissance de Dieu; foi chrétienne et théologie naturelle* (Paris, 1967); H. de Lubac, *Sur les chemins de Dieu* (Paris, 1956).

6. Medellín, "Introduction" 5–6, "Pastoral Care of Elites" 13, "Catechesis" 4, 6; Puebla 15, 28, 797, 997, 1284.

7. Puebla 87–9.

8. Medellín, "Introduction" 5–6, "Pastoral Care of Elites" 13, "Catechesis" 4, 6; Puebla 15, 629, 797–8, 979–82.

9. Medellín, "Poverty of the Church" 7–8; Puebla, "Message" 2–3, 1141–4, 1156.

10. J. B. Libanio and M. C. Bingemer, *Escatologia Cristã* (Petrópolis, 1985).

11. G. E. Wright, *The God Who Acts: Biblical Theology as Recital*

(London and New York, 1962); W. Pannenberg, ed., *Offenbarung als Geschichte* (Göttingen, 1963). Eng. trans.: *Revelation and History* (London, 1965); E. Schillebeeckx, *Revelation and Theology* (London, 1967); R. Latourelle, *Théologie de la révélation* (Bruges, 1963); J. Moltmann, *Theology of Hope* (London and New York, 1967); A. González, *Naturaleza, historia y revelación* (Madrid, 1969).

12. See V. Araya, *God of the Poor* (Maryknoll, N.Y., 1987), with full bibliography.

13. We need to take seriously the challenge posed by Vatican II: "To the extent that they [believers] neglect their own training in the faith, or teach erroneous doctrine, or are deficient in their religious, moral, or social life, they must be said to conceal rather than reveal the authentic face of God and religion" (GS 19).

14. Pss. 10; 14; 73; 94. Cf A. Heschel, *The Prophets*, vol. 2 (New York, 1972), chs. 1–2; L. Sicre, *Los dioses olvidados; poder y riqueza en los profetas preexílicos* (Madrid, 1979); P. Richard, "Biblical Theology of Confrontation with Idols," in Richard et al., *The Idols of Death and the God of Life* (Maryknoll, N.Y., 1983), pp. 3–25; idem, "Raíces idolátricas del pecado social," *Pastoral Popular* 3 (Santiago, Chile, 1983), pp. 43–9.

15. See H. de Lubac, *The Drama of Atheist Humanism* (London, 1949); E. Borne, *Dieu n'est pas mort* (Paris, 1962); K. Rahner, "On the Possibility of Faith," *Theological Investigations*, vol. 5 (London and Baltimore, 1966); H. Cox, *The Secular City* (New York and London, 1967); J. A. T. Robinson, *Honest to God* (London and New York, 1966); E. Schillebeeckx, *God and Man* (London, 1960); idem, *God and the Future of Man* (London, 1973); L. Dewart, *The Future of Belief* (New York and London, 1968); H. Küng, *Does God Exist?* (London and New York, 1983); E. Jüngel, *God as the Mystery of the World* (Edinburgh, 1983); A. Dumas, *Nommer Dieu* (Paris, 1980).

16. CELAM, eds., *Dios: Problemática de la no-creencia en América Latina* (Bogotá, 1974), esp. the contribution by J. Teran Dutari, pp. 75–126.

17. J. Sobrino, "Reflexiones sobre el significado del ateísmo y la idolatría para la teología," RLT 7 (San Salvador, 1986), pp. 45–81.

18. These caricatures and even idols are also found—without doubt—in popular Christianity, as relics of pagan fatalism or submission introjected by the religion of the dominators (see Puebla 308–9, 456, 914, 1069–73).

19. See L. Serenthà, "Dios," *Diccionario teológico interdisciplinar*, vol. 2 (Salamanca, 1983), 263–79; J. Sobrino, "Dios," in C. Floristán and J. Tamayo, eds., *Conceptos fundamentales de pastoral* (Madrid, 1983), 248–64.

II. God on Our Journey in Faith

1. Medellín, "Poverty of the Church" 7–17; Puebla 973–5, 1134–6, 1140, 1147, 1157–8.

2. See S. Galilea, *¿Los pobres nos evangelizan?* (Bogotá, 1980); R. I. de Almeida Cunha, *Opción preferencial por los pobres* (Bogotá, 1981); G. Gutiérrez, "The Irruption of the Poor in Latin America and the Christian Communities of the Common People," in S. Torres and J. Eagleson, eds., *The Challenge of Basic Christian Communities* (Maryknoll, N.Y., 1981), pp. 107–23).

3. See E. Dussel, *Historia general de la iglesia en América Latina,* vol. 1/1 (Salamanca, 1983).

4. J. Sobrino, *The True Church and the Poor* (Maryknoll, N.Y., 1984).

5. See M. Marzal, *Estudios sobre la religión campesina* (Lima, 1977); CELAM, eds., *Iglesia y religiosidad popular en América Latina* (Bogotá, 1977); D. Irarrazával, *Religión del pobre y liberación en Chimbote* (Lima, 1978); P. Suess, *O Catolicismo popular no Brasil* (São Paulo, 1979); F. Castillo, "Christianity: Bourgeois Religion or Popular Religion?" *Concilium* 125 (1979); P. Morande, *Ritual y palabra: Aproximación a la religiosidad popular latinoamericana* (Lima, 1981); S. Galilea, *Religiosidad popular y pastoral* (Madrid, 1980); P. Richard and D. Irarrazával, *Religión y política en América Central: Hacia una nueva interpretación de la religiosidad popular* (San José, 1981); A. Opazo, "Hacia una comprensión teórica de la religión de los oprimidos," *Estudios Sociales Centroamericanas* 33 (San José, 1982); C. Parker, *Religión y clases subalternas urbanas en una sociedad dependiente; religiosidad popular urbana en América Latina: Un estudio de caso en Chile* (Louvain, 1985).

6. J. Comblin, *Antropologia Cristã* (Petrópolis, 1985). Eng. trans.: *Retrieving the Human: A Christian Anthropology* (Maryknoll, N.Y., 1990); *Being Human: A Christian Anthropology* (Tunbridge Wells, 1990), ch. 1.

7. Taller Nueva Historia, *Historia del movimiento obrero* (Santiago, 1983); Grupo de Investigaciones Agrarias, *Historia del movimiento campesino* (Santiago, 1983); D. Camacho, R. Menjivar, eds., *Movimientos populares en Centroamérica* (San José, 1985).

8. C. Parker, "Cristianismo y movimiento popular en Chile," *Plural* 4 (Barcelona, 1985), pp. 9–36; see also A. Opazo, *Función de la iglesia católica en la lucha por la hegemonía en Chile* (Louvain, 1980); J. Osorio and F. Aliaga, "La iglesia chilena y la democracia," *Mensaje* 317 (Santiago, 1983), pp. 95–101.

9. See J. Benoga, *Historia del pueblo mapuche; siglos XIX y XX* (Santiago, 1985); G. Salazar, *Labradores, peones y proletarios: Formación y crisis de la sociedad popular chilena del siglo XIX* (Santiago, 1985).

10. See P. Fontaine, "Liberación y organizaciones populares," *Mensaje* 296 (Santiago, 1981), pp. 14–19; R. Muñoz, "Dejar a la iglesia ser iglesia," *Servicio* 87 (Santiago, 1984), pp. 242–3; F. Castillo, *Iglesia liberadora y política* (Santiago, 1986; Maryknoll, N.Y., forthcoming).

11. See H. Cox, "Seven Samurai and How They Looked Again: Theology, Social Analysis and *Religión popular* in Latin America," in M. Ellis and O. Maduro, eds., *The Future of Liberation Theology: Essays in Honor of Gustavo Gutiérrez* (Maryknoll, N.Y., 1989), pp. 229–39 – TRANS.

12. Two classic texts, one from the second century and one from the twentieth, can be quoted in support: "We [Christians] know that God has no need of any material offerings from men. . . . On the contrary, we know that the only ones pleasing to Him are those that try to imitate the goods proper to Him: temperance, justice, love for his creatures. . . . According to the faith we have received, Christ is the Word (*Logos*) of God of whom all humankind partakes; and so, those who live according to reason (*logos*), though they are considered atheists, are Christians" (St Justin, *Apologia* 1.10.46); "If I lack love or if I lack justice, I distance myself inevitably from you, O God, and my worship is no more than idolatry. To believe in you, I must believe in love and justice, and it is a thousand times better to believe in these things than to pronounce your name. Apart from these it is impossible to meet you at any time, and those who take them as their guide are on the road that leads to you" (H. de Lubac, *Sur les chemins de Dieu* [Paris, 1956]).

13. See John Paul II, *Populorum Progressio* (1967); Medellín, "Justice and Peace"; Puebla 26–62; John Paul II, *Redemptor Hominis* (1979), 13–17. Also, G. Gutiérrez, "The Violence of a System," and E. Dussel, "Relations between Ethics and Economics," both in *Concilium* 140 (1980); P. Richard, "Las Iglesias en el conflicto norte-sur," *Pastoral Popular* 3 (1984), pp. 35–41.

14. For a view of actions and reflections in an industrial, First World society, see R. McAfee Brown, "Reflections of a North American: The Future of Liberation Theology," in Ellis and Maduro, *The Future,* pp. 491–501 – TRANS.

15. See L. Boff, *La experiencia de Dios* (Bogotá, 1977), pp. 43–50; A. Paoli, *El rostro del hermano* (Salamanca, 1979); J. Sobrino, S. Galilea, and A. Castillo, *Oración cristiana y liberación* (Bilbao, 1980); R. Muñoz, "Humanismo evangélico," in *Evangelio y liberación en América Latina* (Santiago and Bogotá, 1980); E. Bonnin, ed., *Espiritualidad y liberación en América Latina* (San José, 1982); P. Casaldáliga, *Experiencia de Dios y pasión por el pueblo: Escritos pastorales.* (Santander, 1983); J. Hourton, "Enrique Alvear, en la búsqueda de Dios," *Mensaje* 317

(Santiago, 1983), pp. 103–6; G. Gutiérrez, *We Drink from Our Own Wells: The Spiritual Journey of a People* (Maryknoll, N.Y., 1984); R. Muñoz, "Llamados de Dios desde el pueblo," *Pastoral Popular* 2 (Santiago, 1984), pp. 2–12; A. Moser, "The Representation of God in the Ethic of Liberation," *Concilium* 172 (1984), pp. 42–7; C. Maccise, *Espiritualidad bíblica en Puebla: Dios presente en la historia* (Bogotá, 1984); S. Galilea, *El camino de la espiritualidad* (Bogotá, 1985); idem, *El futuro de nuestro pasado* (Madrid, 1985). Eng. trans.: *The Future of Our Past* (Quezon City, 1987); various, *Espiritualidad hoy,* entire edition of *Diakonía* 33 (Managua, 1985).

16. See L. Boff, *Teología del cautiverio y de la liberación* (Madrid, 1977); J. Míguez Bonino, *La fe en busca de eficacia* (Salamanca, 1977); G. Gutiérrez, "Desde el reverso de la historia," *La fuerza histórica de los pobres* (Lima, 1979), pp. 303–94. Eng. trans.: *The Power of the Poor in History* (Maryknoll, N.Y., 1983); J. Sobrino, *Resurrección de la verdadera Iglesia* (Salamanca, 1981), pp. 21–53 Eng. trans.: *The True Church and the Poor* (Maryknoll, N. Y., 1984); L. Boff, "Teología de la liberación: Lo mínimo de lo mínimo," in L. Boff and C. Boff, *Libertad y liberación* (Salamanca, 1982); J. I. González Faus, "Los pobres como lugar teológico," RLT 3 (San Salvador, 1984), pp. 275–308; G. Gutiérrez, "Speaking about God," *Concilium* 171 (1984), pp. 27–31; V. Codina, "La irrupción de los pobres en la teología contemporánea," in *De la modernidad a la solidaridad* (Lima, 1984), pp. 17–33; G. Gutiérrez, *On Job: God-Talk and the Suffering of the Innocent* (Maryknoll, N.Y., 1987); idem, *The Truth Shall Make You Free* (Maryknoll, N.Y., 1990).

17. See J. Comblin, *Jesús de Nazaret: meditación sobre la vida y acción humana de Jesús* (Santander, 1977). Eng. trans.: *Jesus of Nazareth* (Maryknoll, N.Y., 1979); R. Vidales, *Desde la tradición de los pobres* (Mexico, 1978), pp. 61–165; H. Echegaray, *La práctica de Jesús* (Lima, 1980). Eng. trans.: *The Practice of Jesus* (Maryknoll, N.Y., and Melbourne, 1984); E. Alvear, "Evangelización liberadora y conflicto," in *El Señor me envió a evangelizar a los pobres* (Santiago, 1983), pp. 49–64; J. Sobrino, *Jesús en América Latina* (San Salvador, 1982), pp. 71–94. Eng. trans.: *Jesus in Latin America* (Maryknoll, N.Y., 1983).

18. Among the texts found most useful in the base communities are Acts 2:42–7; 4:23–37; 11; 1 Cor. 9:26–9; Rev. 2–3.

19. See CLAR, *Pueblo de Dios y comunidad liberadora* (Bogotá, 1977); L. Boff, *Ecclesiogenesis: The Base Communities Reinvent the Church* (Maryknoll, N.Y., 1987); Sobrino, *Resurrección,* pp. 99–142; R. Muñoz, *La iglesia en el pueblo* (Lima, 1983), pp. 97–121; C. Mesters, "Os conflitos no libro dos Atos dos Apóstolos," REB 175 (Petrópolis, 1984), pp. 21–34; E. Hoornaert, *A Memória do povo Cristão* (Petrópolis,

1986). Eng. trans.: *The Memory of the Christian People* (Maryknoll, N.Y., and Tunbridge Wells, 1989).

20. Sobrino, *Resurrección,* pp. 143–76; I. Ellacuria, *Conversión de la iglesia al reino de Dios* (Santander, 1984), pp. 129–216; J. I. González Faus, "Los pobres como lugar teológico," RLT 3 (San Salvador, 1984), pp. 275–308.

21. On ecclesial communion, see Medellín, "Overall Pastoral Approach" 10; Puebla 640–43; on the liberation of the oppressed, see Puebla 28–44, 321–9, 1134–6; Medellín, "Introduction" 5–6.

PART TWO: GOD SEEN FROM OUR SITUATION

Introduction: Cultural Processes and the Christian Experience of God

1. See A. J. Heschel, *The Prophets,* vol. 2 (New York, 1972); W. Pannenberg, *Basic Questions in Theology,* 3 vols. (London, 1970–73).

2. K. Rahner, *The Trinity* (London and Freiburg, 1975).

3. See M. Salinas and J. Irarrazával, *Hacia una teología de los pobres* (Lima, 1980); M. Salinas, "Dos modelos de lectura teológica de la historia latinoamericana," *Pastoral Popular* 1 (Santiago, 1984), pp. 59–65.

4. L. Boff, *Church: Charism and Power* (New York and London, 1985), ch. 2.

5. See S. Galilea, *Pastoral (religiosidad) popular y urbana en América Latina* (Bogotá, 1977); J. L. Caravias, *Religiosidad campesina y liberación* (Bogotá, 1978); CLAR, *Cultura, evangelización y vida religiosa* (Bogotá, 1981); G. Quiroz, *Evangelización y cultura campesina* (Santiago, n.d.).

6. E. Vale, *Juventud, análisis de una opción* (Bogotá, 1982); E. Valenzuela, *La rebelión de los jóvenes; un estudio sobre anomia social* (Santiago, 1984).

III. God and the World

1. On the creation narratives, see C. Hauret, *Origines de l'univers et de l'homme (Genèse I–III),* 2d ed. (Paris, 1950); H. Renckens, *Israel's Concept of the Beginning: The Theology of Genesis I–III* (New York, 1964); G. Auzou, *La tradition biblique: Histoire des écrits sacrés* (Paris, 1957); G. von Rad, *Genesis: A Commentary* (London, 1969); J. Severino Croatto, *El hombre en el mundo* (Buenos Aires, 1974).

2. G. von Rad, *Old Testament Theology,* 2 vols. (Edinburgh and London, 1962, 1965).

3. M. Salinas, "Dos modelos de lectura teológica de la historia latinoamericana," *Pastoral Popular* 1 (Santiago, 1984), pp. 59–65.

4. See J. Severino Croatto, *Liberación y libertad; pautas hermenéu-ticas* (Buenos Aires, 1973); C. Mesters, *El misterioso mundo de la Biblia* (Buenos Aires, 1977); E. Tamez, *Bible of the Oppressed* (Maryknoll, N.Y., 1981); C. Mesters, *Flor sem defesa; uma explicaçãao da Biblia a partir do povo* (Petrópolis, 1983). Eng. trans.: *Defenseless Flower: A New Reading of the Bible* (Maryknoll, N.Y., 1990); C. Mesters, et al., "A Biblia como memória dos pobres," REB 173 (1984); A. Anderson, et al., "Camino de libertação," REB 174 (1984).

5. It is worth observing here that the term "hierarchy" (sacred power), which has since the Middle Ages been so important in the self-understanding and internal organization of the Roman Catholic Church, does not derive from the New Testament, but from Platonism and Eastern mysticism—particularly the Gnostic currents—in accord with the "monarchianism" (central power of one person) of the Roman Empire. See J. Colson, "Hiérarchie," in the dictionary *Catholicisme,* vol. 5 (Paris, 1962), 715–20; P. Eicher, "Hierarchie," *Neues Handbuch theologischer Grundbegriffe,* vol. 2 (Munich, 1984), pp. 177–96; E. Peterson, "Der Monotheismus als politisches Problem," *Theologische Trak-tate* (Munich, 1951), pp. 45–149. This is not the place to argue the need for and basis of pastoral authority in the Christian church. In any case, this authority can be posited and practised *evangelically* only as a "ministry," as humble service in the bosom of the community of brothers and sisters (see Matt. 20:20–28; 23:6–12; Luke 22:24–7; John 13:12–17).

6. For a detailed presentation and systematic reflection on this aspect, see L. Boff, *Trinity and Society* (Tunbridge, and Maryknoll, N.Y., 1988).

IV. God and Human Beings

1. "Pelagianism" is the teaching of Pelagius, Augustine's contemporary. Augustine accused him of accentuating the importance of human freedom and will in achieving salvation, to the detriment of the saving action of God's grace.

2. So Paul VI was able to say that if the Second Vatican Council was able to speak to us today as we are, if it sought no more than to serve human beings, this did not mean that it had turned away from God: on the contrary, it meant that it had been converted to God. The Christian religion is that of service to and love for our fellows—especially the poor—in whom it recognizes the face of Christ. See "Closing Messages of the Council," 8 Dec. 1965, in W. Abbott, ed., *The Documents of Vatican II* (Washington and London-Dublin, 1966). At the same time, sacramental signs and liturgical celebration play an impor-

tant role in the church of Jesus Christ, and have a Christian significance in the lives of the people and in the church's service to them. See L. Boff, *Los sacramentos de la vida y la vida de los sacramentos* (Bogotá, 1975); C. Floristán and L. Maldonado, *Los sacramentos, signos de liberación* (Madrid, 1977); F. Taborda, *Sacramentos, práxis e festa* (Petrópolis, 1987). For a critique of the ahistorical language of the present Roman liturgy, see C. Duquoc and J. Guichard, *Política y vocabulario litúrgico* (Santander, 1977).

3. The beatitudes in Matthew (5:1–12) are precisely this: a summing up of the good news of the Kingdom preached by Jesus, as joyful witness to his own liberating (messianic) practice and the way he offered his disciples; a proclamation of the joy offered to God's children, brought about in practice by the Christian community, proclaimed in turn by the evangelist who is part of that community. See J. Dupont, *Les béatitudes,* vol. 3 (Paris, 1973), pt. 2.

4. See Y. Congar, "La miséricorde, attribut souverain de Dieu," in *Les voies du Dieu vivant* (Paris, 1962), pp. 61–74.

5. This is not calling into question the biblical theology of expiatory sacrifice, applied to the death of Christ principally by reference to the fourth song of the Suffering Servant in Isaiah 52:13 – 53:12. I am simply reporting the viewpoint and accents in the perception of faith by these Christian communities, which contrast with the "theological theory" (medieval in origin) or "ideology" aforementioned. See L. Boff, *Teología del cautiverio y de la liberación* (Madrid, 1977), pp. 179–204.

6. See J. Schmitt, *Jésus réssucité dans la prédication apostolique* (Paris, 1969); C. H. Dodd, *The Apostolic Preaching and Its Development* (London, 1936).

7. See, e.g., St Irenaeus, *Adversus haereses* 2.1.1; Origen, *Contra Celsum* 4.7–8.62–75.

8. See L. Maldonado, *La violencia de lo sagrado* (Salamanca, 1974); idem, *El misterio del mundo: Claves para una interpretación antropológica* (Salamanca, 1982); J. González Faus, "Violencia, religión, sociedad y cristología. Introducción a la obra de R. Girard," *Actualidad Bibliográfica* 35 (Barcelona, 1981), pp. 7–37.

9. See A. Heschel, *The Prophets,* vol. 2 (New York, 1972); W. Pannenberg, *Basic Questions in Theology,* 3 vols. (London, 1970–73); J. Moltmann, *Theology of Hope* (London and New York, 1967).

10. See J. B. Metz, ed., *Christianity and the Bourgeoisie* (*Concilium* 125, 1979); R. Vidales, *Cristianismo anti-burgués* (San José, 1978); V. Codina, *Renacer a la solidaridad* (Santander, 1982).

PART III: BIBLICAL REFLECTION

Introduction: Biblical Revelation and Our Experience of God

1. See H. Gressmann, *Mose und seine Zeit* (1913), quoted in A. Alt, "The God of the Fathers," in *Essays on Old Testament History and Religion* (Oxford, 1966), pp. 1–66.
2. See Alt, "God of the Fathers."
3. See N. Lohfink, *Great Themes from the Old Testament* (Edinburgh, 1982); for a further examination of the God of Abraham, see A. MacKenzie, "God: Power or Personality?" in *Faith and History in the Old Testament* (Minneapolis, 1963), pp. 18–31; A. González, *Abraham, padre de los creyentes* (Madrid, 1963).
4. K. Rahner, "*Theos* in the New Testament," *Theological Investigations*, vol. 1 (London and Baltimore, 1961), 79–149.

V. The God of the Old Testament

1. "Novum Testamentum in veteri velabatur, vetus Testamentum in novo revelatur" (*Sermo 160* 6, PL 38, 876).
2. See L. Larcher, *L'actualité chrétienne de l'Ancien Testament d'après le Nouveau Testament* (Paris, 1962); P. Grelot, *Sens chrétien de l'Ancien Testament* (Paris, 1966).
3. K. Rahner, "*Theos* in the New Testament," *Theological Investigations*, vol. 1 (London and Baltimore, 1961), pp. 92–4.
4. Outstanding examples of this approach are: J. L. Segundo, "Etapas precristianas de la fe," in *¿Qué es un cristiano?* (Montevideo, 1971), pp. 5–85; C. Mesters, *Deus, onde estás?* (Belo Horizonte, 1976).
5. See T. Vriezen, *An Outline of Old Testament Theology* (Oxford, 1958), pp. 128–36.
6. See R. Otto, *Lo santo* (Madrid, 1965); G. van der Leeuw, *Fenomenología de la religión* (Mexico, 1964); J. Martín Velasco, *Introducción a la fenomenología de la religión* (Madrid, 1978).
7. See B. Renaud, *Je suis un Dieu jaloux* (Paris, 1963); G. von Rad, *Old Testament Theology*, vol. 1 (Edinburgh and London, 1962), pp. 203–12.
8. On God's justice, mercy and faithfulness in the Old Testament, see, e.g., A. Heschel, *The Prophets*, vol. 2 (New York, 1972), chs. 4–7; J. Guillet, *Thèmes bibliques* (Paris, 1951); E. Jacob, *Teología del Antiguo Testamento* (Madrid, 1969), pt. 1, chs. 7–9; W. Eichrodt, *Theology of the Old Testament*, vol. 1 (London, 1961), ch. 7.

9. On the God of the poor, see, e.g., J. Dupont, *Les béatitudes,* vol. 2 (Paris, 1969), chs. 1–3; V. Araya, *God of the Poor* (Maryknoll, N.Y., 1987); M. Díaz Mateos, *El Dios que libera* (Lima, 1985), pt. 1; G. Gutiérrez, *On Job: God-Talk and the Suffering of the Innocent* (Maryknoll, N.Y., 1987), pt. 2.

10. Vriezen, *An Outline,* pp. 169–75; J. Guillet, "Le titre biblique Dieu Vivant," in various, *L'homme devant Dieu* (Paris, 1963), pp. 11–23.

11. On the name and names of God, see, e.g., E. Jacob, *Teología del Antiguo Testamento* (Madrid, 1969), pt. 1, ch. 2; A. Besnard, *Le mystère du nom* (Paris, 1962); Eichrodt, *Theology,* vol. 1, ch. 5; von Rad, *Old Testament Theology,* vol. 1, pp. 203–12.

12. See Heschel, *The Prophets,* vol. 2, chs. 6–7; F. Michaeli, *Dieu à l'image de l'homme* (Neuchâtel, 1950); Vriezen, *An Outline,* pp. 172–3; J. Briend, "Parler humainement de Dieu: Anthropomorphisme et alterité de Dieu dans l'Ancien Testament," *Lumière et Vie* 128 (1976), pp. 7–19.

VI. The God of Jesus of Nazareth

1. See X. Léon Dufour, "The Synoptic Gospels," in A. Robert and A. Feuillet, eds., *Introduction to the Old Testament,* vol. 2 (New York, 1968); B. Gerhardsson, *The Origins of the Gospel Traditions* (London, 1974).

2. See I. Ortiz de Urbina, *Nicea y Constantinopla* (Vitoria, 1969), pp. 69–92, 183–205; J. Kelly, *Early Christian Creeds* (London, 1972).

3. The following exposition owes much to J. Guillet, "Genèse de la foi chez les apôtres," *Christus* 46 (1955), pp. 177–94.

4. See J. Comblin, *La oración de Jesús* (Santiago, n.d.); J. Sobrino, *Cristología desde América Latina* (Mexico, 1977), pp. 109–34. Eng. trans.: *Christology at the Crossroads* (Maryknoll, N.Y. and London, 1978).

5. See T. W. Manson, *The Teaching of Jesus* (Cambridge, 1959), pp. 89–115; J. Jeremias, *The Central Meaning of the New Testament* (London, 1965).

VII. God in the New Testament Message

1. K. Rahner, "*Theos* in the New Testament," *Theological Investigations,* vol. 1 (London and Baltimore, 1961).

2. Rahner, "*Theos*"; B. Lonergan, *De Verbo Incarnato,* thesis prima (Rome, 1961); J. Kelly, *Early Christian Creeds* (London, 1972); L. Boff,

Trinity and Society (Tunbridge Wells and Maryknoll, N.Y., 1988), ch. 4.

3. Cf Rahner, *"Theos"*; M. Löhrer, "Observations dogmatiques sur la question des propriétés et formes d'actuer de Dieu," *Mysterium Salutis,* vol. 5 (Paris, 1970).

Select Bibliography

Andrade, B. *Encuentro con Dios en la historia: Estudio de la concepción de Dios en el Pentateuco.* Salamanca: Sígueme, 1985.

Araya, V. *God of the Poor.* Maryknoll, N.Y.: Orbis, 1987. See the abundant bibliography.

Boff, L. *La experiencia de Dios.* 2d ed. Bogotá: CLAR, 1977.

———. *Jesus Christ Liberator.* Maryknoll, N.Y.: Orbis, 1978.

———. *The Lord's Prayer.* Maryknoll, N.Y.: Orbis, 1984.

———. *Passion of Christ, Passion of the World.* Maryknoll, N.Y.: Orbis, 1987.

Deissler, A. "La révélation personelle de Dieu dans l'Ancien Testament." In *Mysterium Salutis,* vol. 5. Paris, 1970.

Díaz Mateos, M. *El Dios que libera.* Lima: CEP, 1985, pt. 2.

Didier, M. "La révélation de Dieu par Jésus Christ." In various, *Croire en Dieu aujourd'hui?* Gembloux: Duculot, 1986, pp. 26–55.

Dupont, J. *Les béatitudes.* Vols. 2 and 3. Paris: Gabalda, 1969, 1973.

Duquoc, C. *Dieu différent.* Paris: Cerf, 1977.

Echegaray, H. *The Practice of Jesus.* Maryknoll, N.Y.: Orbis; Melbourne: Dove, 1984.

Eichrodt, W. *Theology of the Old Testament.* 2 vols. London: SCM Press, 1961, 1967.

Fackenheim, E. L. *God's Presence in History: Jewish Affirmations and Philosophical Reflections.* New York: New York University Press, 1970.

García Murga, J. R. "El rostro liberador de Dios." In A. Vargas Machuca, ed., *Teología y mundo contemporáneo.* Madrid: Cristiandad, 1975, pp. 89–114.

Gerstenberger, G., ed. *Deus no Antigo Testamento.* São Paulo: ASTE, 1981.

González Faus, J. I. "¿Qué Dios se nos revela en Jesucristo?" *Diakonía* 17 (Managua, 1981), pp. 23–38.

González Faus, J. I., and J. Vives. *Creer sólo se puede en Dios; en Dios sólo se puede creer.* Santander: Sal Terrae, 1985.

González Ruiz, J. M. *Dios es gratuito pero no superfluo.* Madrid: Marova, 1971.

Gutiérrez, G. *The God of Life.* Maryknoll, N.Y.: Orbis, forthcoming.

——. *On Job: God-Talk and the Suffering of the Innocent.* Maryknoll, N.Y.: Orbis, 1987.

——. *The Power of the Poor in History.* Maryknoll, N.Y.: Orbis, 1983.

——. *We Drink from Our Own Wells: The Spiritual Journey of a People.* Maryknoll, N.Y.: Orbis; Melbourne: Dove, 1984.

Heschel, A. J. *The Prophets.* 2 vols. New York: Harper and Row, 1969, 1972.

Jeremias, J. *The Central Message of the New Testament.* London: SCM, 1965.

——. *New Testament Theology. Part One: The Proclamation of Jesus.* London: SCM, 1971.

Manson, T. W. *The Teaching of Jesus.* Cambridge, Eng.: CUP, 1959.

Mesters, C. *Deus, onde estás?* Belo Horizonte: Vega, 1976.

Moltmann, J. *The Crucified God.* 5th ed. London: SCM, 1985.

Muñoz, R. *Evangelio y liberación en América Latina.* Santiago and Bogotá: CLAR, 1980.

——. *Nueva conciencia de la iglesia en América Latina.* Salamanca: Sígueme, 1974.

Rad, G. von. *Old Testament Theology.* 2 vols. Edinburgh and London: Oliver and Boyd, 1962, 1965.

Rahner, K. "*Theos* in the New Testament." In *Theological Investigations,* vol. 1. London: Darton, Longman and Todd; Baltimore: Helicon, 1961, pp. 79–149.

Rovira, J. M. *Revelación de Dios, salvación del hombre.* Salamanca: Secretariado Trinitario, 1979.

Schäfer, K. "Jesus' Witness to God." *Concilium* 76 (1972).

Schillebeeckx, E. "The 'God of Jesus' and the 'Jesus of God.' " *Concilium* 93 (1974).

Segundo, J. L. *¿Qué es un cristiano?* Montevideo: Mosca, 1971.

——. *A Theology for Artisans of a New Humanity.* Vol. 3: *Our Idea of God.* Maryknoll, N.Y.: Orbis, 1974.

Sobrino, J. *Christology at the Crossroads.* Maryknoll, N.Y.: Orbis; London: SCM, 1978, chs. 3 and 4.

——. "Cómo abordar pastoralemnte el tema Dios." *Fe y Solidaridad* 44 (Santiago, 1983).

——. "Dios." In C. Floristán and J. Tamayo, eds., *Conceptos fundamentales de pastoral.* Madrid: Cristiandad, 1983, pp. 248–64.

——. "Dios de vida, urgencia y solidaridad." *Diakonía* 35 (Managua, 1985), pp. 232–52.

——. "Dios y los procesos revolucionarios." In various, *Apuntes para una teología nicaragüense.* San José: DEI-CAV, 1981, pp. 105–29.

——. "Reflexiones sobre el significado del ateísmo y la idolatría para la teología." RLT 7 (San Salvador, 1986), pp. 45–81.

——. "Jesus' Proclamation of the Reign of God: Importance for Today," *Spirituality of Liberation* (Maryknoll, N.Y.: Orbis, 1988), pp. 117–31.

——. *The True Church and the Poor.* Maryknoll, N.Y.: Orbis, 1984.

Thüsing, W., and K. Rahner. *A New Christology.* London: Burns and Oates, 1980.

Various. *La cultura popular como espiritualidad de la liberación.* Entire edition of *Christus* 567–8 (Mexico, 1983).

——. *Dios de vida, ídolos de muerte.* Entire edition of *Misión Abierta* 5–6 (Madrid, 1985).

——. *Espiritualidad hoy.* Entire edition of *Diakonía* 33 (Managua, 1985).

——. *Experimentar Deus hoje.* Petrópolis: Vozes, 1976.

——. *La lucha de los dioses.* San José: DEI, 1980.

——. *La palabra hecha con la vida.* Entire edition of *Christus* 591–2 (Mexico, 1985–6).

Vriezen, T. *An Outline of Old Testament Theology.* Oxford: Blackwell, 1958, pp. 128–98.

Wright, G. E. *The God Who Acts: Biblical Theology as Recital.* London: Duckworth; New York: Doubleday, 1962.

Index

Books of general Christian interest as well as books on theology, scripture, spirituality and mysticism are published by Burns and Oates Limited.

A free catalogue will be sent on request:

BURNS AND OATES Dept A,

Wellwood, North Farm Road, Tunbridge Wells, Kent TN2 3DR

Already published in this series

THE HOLY SPIRIT AND LIBERATION

José Comblin

The Holy Spirit is the "great unknown" of Western Theology and one of the great re-discoveries of liberation theology. Few books, however, have yet given it the attention and analysis it deserves. This volume remedies this defect, and in a fresh and challenging way.

Christianity, Comblin argues, has two sources: the "Jesus event" and the coming of the Spirit: Easter and Pentecost. Yet Western tradition has consistently undervalued the place of the Holy Spirit, substituting the chain "Father-Son-Church" for the Trinitarian order, and invoking the Spirit only as a prop for decisions already taken by a hierarchical church.

Finally, he puts forward a new model of spirituality, a spirituality of austerity, commitment and action, finding God in service to the poor, but shot through with "joy in the Spirit".

"Liberation theology can be methodical or charismatic: Comblin is methodical. He has lived for many years in a poor peasant community in Brazil and writes in Portuguese, but his intellect is still that of a member of the faculty at the Catholic University of Louvain. The mix works well. . . . His books are a record of his methodical reflection on this experience (of the Holy Spirit at work in Latin America), replete with scholarship and the fruits of wide reading and careful thought, but driven by the dreadful realities of daily life, the life of the oppressed, the non-persons of the world he lives in. . . . He speaks always from within history and the institutional Church. His is a complete theological vision, alive in contemporary history." – John Todd in *The Tablet*

"This is one of the most remarkable books to come from Latin America; a serious yet accessible theological study." – *Renew*

"This is one of the most stimulating and hopeful books that I have read in a very long time. . . ." – Michael Williams in *Anvil*

THE BIBLE, THE CHURCH AND THE POOR
Jorge Pixley and Clodovis Boff

The subject of the book, the authors tell us in their opening sentence, is the 'option for the poor'. A thorny subject indeed for it is controversial and profoundly challenging for the Churches and is fraught with misunderstanding and even at times deliberate distortion. Throughout the book they face these difficulties with integrity, sureness and originality. As it unfolds we are put in touch with the fruits of Liberation Theology's twenty-year stuggle to find an adequate religious response to the majority of human beings who are poor.

"A sustained and thoughtful examination of the 'preferential option for the poor' by two distinguished Latin American theologians. The importance of the book is underlined by the fact that Pixley is a well-known Protestant biblical scholar, while Clodovis Boff is a Roman Catholic religious from Brazil whose main contributions have been in the area of the methodology of Liberation Theology. Particularly impressive in this book is the careful analysis of the biblical material which is scholarly, committed and honest. . . . What is particularly interesting and impressive in this book is that two very different theological approaches lead to virtually identical conclusions. . . ." – Duncan B Forrester in *The Expository Times*

"The publication of this book will not bring debate about the 'option for the poor' to an end but it will inform and enlighten the contribution of those who read it. I recommend it." – Eamonn Bredin in *The Furrow*

"Pixley and Boff write with clarity and power and with the authority of those who work with the poor as well as theologizing about them." – John Pridmore in *The Way*

"Sound theology and informed historic understanding are basic ingredients. A clear picture of the awful mess we have arrived at in the present phase of human development is tempered by a full awareness that we are process; we do have the means to sort out the mess and to proceed with human progress. This is a fine text and may well become a standard reference book on the topic." – Frances O'Kelly in *The Teilhard Review*